Readings in Government and Ethics
FP 130
United States Naval Academy
Department of Political Science

American Heritage

THOMSON

★

™

LEARNING

For more information, contact Thomson Learning Custom Publishing, 5101 Madison Road, Cincinnati, OH 45227, or electronically at http://www.itpcustomsolutions.com

Thomson Learning Publishing Europe
Berkshire House 168-173
High Holborn
London, WC1V 7AA, England

Thomas Nelson Australia
102 Dodds Street
South Melbourne 3205
Victoria, Australia

Nelson Canada
1120 Birchmount Road
Scarborough, Ontario
Canada M1K 5G4

Thomson Learning Publishing GmbH
Königswinterer Strasse 418
53227 Bonn, Germany

Thomson Learning Editores
Campos Eliseos 385, Piso 7
Col. Polanco
11560 México D.F. México

Thomson Learning Publishing Asia
221 Henderson Road
#05-10 Henderson Building
Singapore 0315

Thomson Learning Publishing Japan
Hirakawacho Kyowa Building, 3F
2-2-1 Hirakawacho
Chiyoda-ku, Tokyo 102, Japan

Thomson Learning Publishing Southern Africa
Building 18, Constantia Park
240 Old Pretoria Road
Halfway House, 1685 South Africa

ISBN 0-324-06731-3

ACKNOWLEDGMENTS

"A Tub to the Whale: The Adoption of the Bill of Rights," by Kenneth R. Bowling. Chapter 3 from, *The Bill of Rights and the States*, edited by Patrick T. Conley and John P. Kaminski. Reprinted with permission from Madison House Publishers, Inc.

"Reflections on the Bicentennial of the United States Constitution," by Thurgood Marshall.101 Harvard Law Review 1, 1-5, 1987. Reprinted with permission from the Journal of the Early Republic.

TABLE OF CONTENTS

CHAPTER 1

NATURE'S GOD AND
THE FOUNDING FATHERS

E. M. Halliday

In this article, Halliday describes the intellectual atmosphere that influenced the thinking of our "Founding Fathers." Though our Founding Fathers shared no specific religious or philosophical outlook, they were " . . . children of the Age of Reason" or the European Enlightenment. Enlightenment thinking made reason its guide and decried any form of absoultism. Respect for dissenting opinion and for man's good nature (directed by innate moral sense or conscience) led our Founding Fathers to promote principles like majority rule and separation of church and state. Halliday's article raises important questions about the assumptions and beliefs our Founding Fathers held regarding people and government. These beliefs are challenged today particularly by those who feel that American society accepts moral relativism and therefore lacks standards.

From his pulpit in Christ Episcopal Church in Philadelphia, Dr. James Abercrombie looked out at a congregation that included the first President of the United States. He had good reason to feel some nervousness on this particular Sunday morning, for he was about to perform an act of ecclesiastical daring. He was about to scold George Washington, in public, for his religious behavior.

Dr. Abercrombie mentioned no names as he pitched into a sermon on the grave responsibility of "those in elevated stations" to set good examples for lesser folk, but only the children in his pews that day could have missed the point. He focused on the celebration of the Lord's Supper; and everyone knew that President Washington habitually joined those who walked out of church, on communion Sundays, just before the sacrament was to be administered. The rector's target was embarrassingly clear.

No doubt Dr. Abercrombie hoped to achieve the pious triumph of persuading the President to take holy communion at his altar. But, although his message had not passed the presidential ears unheeded, the outcome was disconcerting. Washington never again left the church just before the Lord's Supper—from that time forward he did not come at all on communion Sundays.

The minister swallowed his disappointment as best he could. Writing, years later, to someone who had inquired about Washington's religion, he said that according to one of the President's acquaintances—he could not remember precisely whom—the great man preferred to stay away rather than become a communicant because, "were he to become one then, it would be imputed to an ostentatious display of religious zeal." This was a relatively consoling explanation, but there are signs that it failed to convince Dr. Abercrombie himself. "That Washington was a professing Christian," he added to his correspondent, "is evident from his regular attendance in our church, but sir, I cannot consider any man as a real Christian who uniformly disregards an ordinance so solemnly enjoined by the divine Author of our holy religion. . . . "

What were Washington's reasons for refusing to partake in the Lord's Supper? Exact answers are lost to history, concealed behind the reticence he steadily maintained where his private beliefs were concerned. In terms of reasonable inference, however, it is possible to offer an explanation. He had long been exposed to the ideas of the European Enlightenment, and his behavior suggests that his religious views were considerably shaped thereby. It was an intellectual atmosphere not favorable to symbolic rites, among other things. In his exposure to it, Washington was of course far from unique among the Founding Fathers of the American republic. Inevitably, all of his educated contemporaries were to some extent children of the Age of Reason (as Tom Paine called it); and among them several of the acknowledged political leaders were certainly its eminent sons.

Still, there was no great uniformity of opinion among the Founding Fathers on specific religious or philosophical questions. Whether one considers the signers of the Declaration of Independence or the delegates to the Constitutional Convention of 1787, or both, it is easy to find a diversity of sects and creeds. But the broad spectrum of denominations is itself a reminder that a prime characteristic of the Enlightenment was respect for dissenting opinions. The famous remark attributed to Voltaire, "I may disagree with what you say, but I will defend to the death your right to say it," catches the spirit of the era. While full freedom of belief was not legally protected in any of the colonies at the start of the Revolution, and most of them had an established church supported by the government, minority groups and nonconforming individuals were in fact granted considerable leeway. Catholics were strong in Maryland; Quakers, in Pennsylvania. In New England, the evolution of Congregational doctrine had moved toward freedom of conscience for more than a century, so that there was a kind of paradox in the legal establishment of a church so nearly democratic in its organization. The supremacy of the Anglicans in the South, moreover, was weakened by the fact that theirs was the official church of England in a period when independence from the mother country was about to become the paramount fact of current history. For, whatever their doctrinal differences in religion, all of the Founding Fathers were political revolutionaries, determined to enact a new formulation of the idea of government by consent of the governed.

Even Washington's most ardent admirers have never claimed that he was, philosophically, a deep thinker. Thomas Jefferson, by contrast, was as philosophically inclined, and gifted with as keen an analytical mind, as any American of his time. His interest in religion and its proper relationship to government was intense, and it persisted throughout his long life. During his second term as President (1805–1809) he sought relief from the tremendous pressures of his office by composing, for his own satisfaction, a version of the New Testament which he called "The Life and Morals of Jesus of Nazareth." It would have interested Washington, for among many other significant omissions it pointedly left out the story of the Last Supper. This was as good a clue as any to Jefferson's idea in undertaking the work, which was, in his own sharp language, to rescue from "the speculations of crazy theologists" the moral teachings of Jesus, "abstracting what is really his from the rubbish in which it is buried."

In his own terms, Jefferson claimed to be a Christian—but he assuredly was not one according to Dr. Abercrombie's standards, or for that matter according to the doctrine of any organized Christian church, unless it was the fledgling Unitarian. He rejected, he wrote, "the immaculate conception of Jesus, his deification, the creation of the world by him, his miraculous powers, his resurrection and visible ascension, his corporeal presence in the Eucharist, the Trinity, original sin, atonement, regeneration, election, orders of Hierarchy, etc." He thought of Christ as a great reformer, author of "a system of the most sublime morality which has ever fallen from the lips of man"—but human rather than divine. To be a Christian, for Jefferson, was simply to follow the system of ethics taught by Christ, uncontaminated by what he considered the additions, adulterations, and distortions of those who came after. And Jefferson thought he had an easy touchstone for distinguishing Jesus' original teachings from the dross. All that was needed was the "free exercise of reason": with that, the genuine precepts of the Master would never be found to disagree.

To orthodox clergymen and theologians this was heresy; it was, many of them angrily charged, a mere disguise for atheism. As a prominent political figure, Jefferson often suffered from his refusal to accept traditional Christianity, even though he tried to keep his religious views largely to himself. His skepticism toward anything alleged to be supernatural was misunderstood, and his high regard for Christian ethics was usually ignored. Shocking stories circulated long before he became a presidential candidate, and their currency grew with his fame. John Trumbull, the great painter of the Revolution, told one about a dinner party at Jefferson's home in 1793, when the future President sat "smiling and nodding approbation" while Congressman William Giles of Virginia—a fellow skeptic— "proceeded so far . . . as to ridicule the character, conduct and doctrines of the divine founder of our religion." This was unquestionably an exaggeration, but it suggests Jefferson's reputation at the time. When he was presidential runner-up in 1796, a minister in Connecticut took note of the event in a prayer before his congregation: "O Lord! wilt Thou bestow upon the Vice President a double portion of Thy grace, for *Thou knowest he needs it.*" In the campaign of 1800 Jefferson's "infidelity" was an easy target for Federalist orators and pamphleteers.

Yet there is little doubt that Jefferson held a profound belief in a Supreme Being. In a fashion typical of eighteenth-century intellectuals, he held it not on implicit faith, but as a reasoned conclusion based on evidence and deduction. "I hold (without appeal to revelation)," he once wrote to John Adams, "that when we take a view of the universe, in its parts, general or particular, it is impossible for the human mind not to perceive and feel a conviction of design, consummate skill, and indefinite power in every atom of its composition." Newton and his contemporaries in the seventeenth century had magnificently demonstrated that man lived in a universe of precise mathematical law and order; it seemed scientifically evident to most thinkers in the following era that such a cosmic design could come only from the hand of a divine Creator.

It was a long way from the theology of traditional Christianity; this idea of an invisible but demonstrable God whose existence was proved only by His handiwork; for "He" was now a nearly impersonal power, responsible for the origin and laws of the universe, but not interfering in its operation once the myriad wheels of the great machine had been set in motion. This was "Nature's God," as Jefferson phrased it in the Declaration of Independence; and to him and many others the religion appropriate to Nature's God must be natural, not supernatural, in its foundations. Deism, or "natural religion," expressed their theological creed, not a Christianity based on revelation, mystery, and miracle.

Some men—notably a prominent group in France including Diderot, d'Alembert, Condorcet, and the Baron d'Holbach—went further, postulating an automatic universe, operating by inexorable natural laws, but utterly devoid of God or God's purpose. Jefferson was inclined to resist this surge toward atheism, yet it is only justice to the true character of his mind to emphasize that his attitude was far from fanatical. He was never an absolutist, even on the question of God's existence. His creed of intellectual freedom was much too firm for that, and at worst he saw no alarming threat in atheism. Before he went to France to be United States minister from 1784 to 1789, he had already considered the effects of full disbelief. "It does me no injury for my neighbor to say there are twenty Gods, or no God," he observed in his *Notes on Virginia* (1782). "It neither picks my pocket nor breaks my leg." And writing to his young nephew, Peter Carr, from Paris in 1787, he urged him to make reason his guide: " . . . call to her tribunal every fact, every opinion. Question with boldness even the existence of a God; because, if there be one, he must more approve of the homage of reason, than that of blindfolded fear."

Jefferson's vital disposition toward freedom of thought was strengthened by his five years in France. Not only was he there a first-hand observer of the moral and material degradation resulting, as he saw it, from the combination of religious persecution and tyrannical government. In that cosmopolitan air he also made familiar contact with many of the most brilliant figures of the age. The political, philosophical, and religious ideas of the Enlightenment now reached him not just in books, but in absorbing conversations across his own dinner table. Voltaire had written that atheists, deplorable as they might be, would still make better neighbors than religious fanatics. Jefferson came to know some of the leading French atheists as friends and acquaintances, and he found them anything but monsters. "Diderot, D'Alembert, D'Holbach, Condorcet," he wrote to a friend years later, "are known to have been among the most virtuous of men. Their virtue, then, must have had some other foundation than the love of God."

This crucial question of the basis of human morality, bearing as it does on the relation between religion and government, intrigued Jefferson all his life. He early formed an opinion consistent with the natural religion of the Enlightenment, and from it he never swerved throughout the remainder of his eighty-three years. Its essence was natural morality. "Man was destined for society," he wrote to his nephew in 1787. " . . . He was endowed with a sense of right and wrong, merely relative to this. This sense is as much a part of his nature, as the sense of hearing, seeing, feeling; it is the true foundation of morality. . . . The moral sense, or conscience, is as much a part of man as his leg or arm." And while Jefferson firmly believed that this moral sense was the gift of a divine Creator, he was equally certain that acknowledgment of its source was not necessary to its function. If young Peter Carr, having fully considered the evidence, were to become an atheist, still, Jefferson assured him, "you will find incitements to virtue in the comfort and pleasantness you feel in its exercise, and the love of others which it will procure you."

Jefferson's theory of natural morality was for him the cornerstone of the democratic faith which he did so much during his lifetime to make a living reality. The church doctrine of original sin was anathema to him. Human nature could be trusted: all normal men were endowed by their Creator not only with unalienable rights, but with unalienable instincts, including a natural moral sense. Except under bad social conditions—ignorance, poor education, poverty—the mass of men, he felt, would surely gravitate toward what was right on fundamental issues, if only they were allowed complete freedom of conscience. The principle of majority rule—a sacred principle to Jefferson—depended on the premise of a well-informed public, each member of which could choose among moral or political alternatives with absolute freedom from mental coercion.

This is the key to Jefferson's lifelong insistence on complete separation of church and state. While it was a matter of democratic principle with him to champion full freedom of voluntary association, so that any number of divergent sects could thrive without government interference, he had no sympathy for their dogmatic approach to questions of moral truth. An organized church, he thought, was unlikely to leave men's minds completely free. Whatever the denomination, each claimed a special revelation of God's will, imparted directly to its prophets or priests, or recorded in the Bible. (Franklin, whose views were much like Jefferson's, said that religious sects reminded him of "a certain French lady who, in a dispute with her sister, said, 'I don't know how it happens, sister, but I meet with nobody but myself that's always in the right!'") Few were therefore willing to relinquish moral (and, by implication, political) choices to the untrammelled conscience of the individual citizen.

Jefferson had the good fortune to live long and to compose his own epitaph after much deliberation. It was a modest statement for a man who had been among the foremost in establishing the American nation. He wished his tombstone to cite him in three capacities only: "Author of the Declaration of American Independence; of the Statute of Virginia for Religious Freedom; and Father of the University of Virginia." The order was chronological, but in a most important sense the three accomplishments were one and indivisible. The Declaration of Independence envisaged a free society ruled by consent of the governed. But informed decision and consent could be based only on good public education; and good education, in turn, could be based only on complete freedom of the mind. In the history of the new republic the first fundamental challenge to freedom of the mind came in the area of religion.

It is a curious fact of American history that the man who was inseparably associated with Jefferson in his fight for religious freedom, and who was to become his closest friend for nearly half a century, grew up only thirty-odd miles from Monticello, yet never met him until late in 1776. James Madison of Montpelier, in Port Conway, Virginia, came to the capitol at Williamsburg in May of that year, an elected delegate to the state convention. By that time, Jefferson was off to his appointment with fame in Philadelphia, and so the two did not meet until the following autumn—and even then their contact was slight. But in the meantime something had happened at Williamsburg to form a bond between them no less strong for its resting temporarily unperceived.

The government of Virginia was in process of being overhauled in the spring of 1776, and although young Madison, a relatively unknown delegate, did not have a great deal to do with the new state constitution, he was a member of a committee appointed to draw up a bill of rights. The great George Mason of Gunston Hall was chief author of the articles in this bill, which was to become the prototype for similar manifestoes in other states as well as, eventually, for the Bill of Rights of the United States Constitution.

It must have cheered Jefferson to see that prominent among the Virginia articles was one on religious freedom. Madison was instrumental in giving that article its final and significant form when the committee proposal went before the Virginia convention on June 12, 1716. Only five years out of college at Princeton, he was already an accomplished student of constitutional law, a man cast very much in Jefferson's mold. As he saw it, Mason's expression of the principle of religious freedom was deficient in two respects: it allowed for continuation of a state-supported church, and it spoke of "toleration in the exercise of religion" rather than absolute freedom of conscience. Recognizing that it was not quite time to push for disestablishment in Virginia, Madison let that go, but proposed a rewording that would move forward from the idea of mere toleration (which implied the right of the state either to grant or withhold religious freedom) to that of freedom of conscience as an unalienable natural right. The convention was not willing to go quite that far, but, in its permanent form, the article pronounced that "all men are equally entitled to the free exercise of religion, according to the dictates of conscience." It was a quiet yet important triumph in the struggle for complete liberty of thought in America.

When he began to become well acquainted with Madison, in the summer of 1779, Jefferson was fresh from a half-successful effort to abolish state sanction of religion in Virginia. Government salaries for Anglican ministers had been suspended, but their church was still functioning as the official one in the state, and other impediments to religious liberty persisted. It was impossible to be legally married, for example, unless the ceremony was performed by an Anglican clergyman, and heresy against the Christian faith was still a crime. Jefferson's comprehensive "Bill for Establishing Religious Freedom" would have swept aside all such restrictions, as well as forbidding government support of any church. But it ran into fierce opposition in the Virginia legislature when it was introduced in June, 1779, and failed to pass.

Nevertheless, the Bill for Religious Freedom must have exerted a strong attractive force between Jefferson and Madison. They were now often in close consultation, Jefferson as newly elected governor, Madison as a member of his executive council; their personal friendship was also growing fast. Although Madison had been, from his college days, more skeptical and less orthodox than he has been painted by many biographers, his commitment to absolute freedom of thought as the undergirding of a free society was henceforth more intense. By the time Jefferson left for France, Madison was well prepared to carry on their campaign not only in Virginia, but in the first Congress, to which he would go as a representative in 1789.

In Virginia, Madison's skill finally brought victory for Jefferson's disestablishment bill, but not without a tough running battle against an opposition headed by the redoubtable Patrick Henry. By 1784 the state Anglican hierarchy was vociferously pressing for new tax funds to support the church, and Henry proposed an annual assessment for "the support of the Christian religion or of some Christian church," without naming any particular sect. This attempted shift from the traditional, single-church form of establishment to the multiple, embracing several denominations, was part of a trend now apparent in more than one of the states of the new nation. It was a type of defensive strategy which would continue for nearly two centuries, as efforts to retain government sanction for religion moved to an ever broader and less sectarian base. In Virginia in 1784 the Presbyterians, hitherto enemies of establishment, now joined the phalanx demanding it in the broader form. They seemed as ready, Madison noted to his friend James Monroe, "to set up an establishment which is to take them in as they were to pull down that which shut them out."

Meanwhile, Madison was by no means impotent on the other side of the issue. He anonymously wrote his now famous "Memorial and Remonstrance Against Religious Assessments" (1785), which was circulated wide and far in Virginia as a petition to which thousands signed their names in protest against the renewed prospect of religious establishment. As copy after copy of the petition, crowded with signatures, streamed into the Virginia Assembly, it became very clear that the majority of the people were in no mood to forsake the religious freedom they had been promised by the 1776 Declaration of Rights. The surprised proponents of the assessment bill never even bothered to bring it to a vote.

Madison's "Remonstrance" was a piece of shrewd political propaganda. It struck a chord more in harmony with the orthodox Christianity of those to whom it was addressed than his private views might have sustained, yet it echoed the rationalist strain of his religious discussions with Jefferson.

In fifteen paragraphs, many of them harking back to the popular article on religion in the 1776 Declaration of Rights, he argued against government support of the church. Every man's religion, he wrote,

> must be left to the conviction and conscience of every man; and it is the right of every man to exercise it as these may dictate. This right is in its nature an unalienable right . . . because the opinions of men, depending only on the evidence contemplated by their own minds, cannot follow the dictates of other men. . . . We maintain therefore that in matters of Religion, no man's right is abridged by the institution of Civil Society, and that Religion is wholly exempt from its cognizance. . . . Who does not see that the same authority which can establish Christianity, in exclusion of all other Religions, may establish with the same ease any particular sect of Christians, in exclusion of all other Sects? . . . Whilst we assert for ourselves a freedom to embrace, to profess, and to observe the Religion which we believe to be of divine origin, we cannot deny an equal freedom to those whose minds have not yet yielded to the evidence which has convinced us. . . .

It is noteworthy, since it bears on the meaning of the First Amendment to the Constitution, that to Madison and the thousands of Virginians who signed his petition, "establishment of religion" meant any government sponsorship of any or all religions, and not just the European pattern of an exclusive, official state church. (The "Remonstrance" refers repeatedly to Henry's general assessment bill as "the proposed establishment.") They wanted a solid "wall of separation between church and state," to use a phrase Jefferson invented later. Acting on the theory that a good time to dispatch an enemy was when he was on the run, Madison and his friends in the legislature now took Jefferson's Bill for Religious Liberty off the shelf where it had seasoned since 1779, and this time saw it voted in by a substantial majority. In principle it was a twin to Madison's "Remonstrance," but even more trenchant in its rhetoric and forthright in its defense of absolute freedom of thought and expression—a forerunner, as well as, in a sense, an interpretation of the First Amendment to the Constitution.

A last-minute effort by the opposition to confine the benefits of the law to Christians instead of protecting even (as Jefferson noted) "the Infidel of every denomination," failed. Early in 1786, Madison was able to send his friend the news that through their collaboration the most sweeping guarantee of freedom of conscience in the history of the western world had become a statute of Virginia. He felt that its provisions, he wrote Jefferson, "have in this country extinguished forever the ambitious hope of making laws for the human mind." Fervently sharing this sentiment, Jefferson saw to it that the new statute was translated into French and Italian, widely published, and "inserted in the new Encyclopedie." He reported "infinite approbation in Europe."

The example of Virginia—by far the largest of the thirteen states in population, and home of a cluster of distinguished men headed by the revered Washington— could hardly be ignored in the rest of America. The winds of revolution already had blown away much restrictive custom and legislation by 1786. Most of the other states had recently passed bills of rights honoring religious freedom, even though, with the exception of Rhode Island, New Jersey, and New York, they still had church establishment in at least the multiple form, embracing several sects. It was to be a number of years before any of them matched Virginia, yet it was natural that her action greatly strengthened the general current toward increased freedom of thought and an accompanying separation of church and state.

But it was to be almost by accident that the question of religious freedom first arose at the national level. The Constitutional Convention, gathering at Philadelphia in the spring of 1787, ignored it for many weeks—not because it was felt to be unimportant, but because it was considered the business of the states rather than of the central government. But as a hot August steamed into a hot September, it became obvious that the federal machinery designed by men like Madison, Alexander Hamilton, and Roger Sherman was far more powerful than the old Articles of Confederation. What about the rights of the people under such a government? They ought to be, asserted George Mason, "the pole star of political conduct." The state governments were, in 1787, the guardians of those rights; but the new Constitution greatly reduced the power of the states. With Mason at the center, a small nucleus of delegates began to agitate for specific guarantees, to be built into the Constitution itself. Charles Pinckney, of South Carolina, urged a ban on religious tests for federal officeholders, and the Convention—thinking, no doubt, of their own wide spread of religious opinion—quickly adopted it (Article VI).

Still, the movement for a full bill of rights, similar to those prevailing in a majority of the states, found little support. Mason was deeply disturbed, and announced that he would "sooner chop off his right hand than put it to the Constitution as it now stands." But Roger Sherman expressed the more general feeling when he said that "the State Declarations of Rights are not repealed by this Constitution; and being in force are sufficient." The tired delegates brought the Convention to a close on September 17, 1787, and the Constitution was submitted to the states without a bill of rights. Mason did not chop off his hand, but he did quit the Convention without signing.

As the contest over ratification swung back and forth in the various state legislatures during 1787–88, the federalists were forced to admit that a compromise was in order. From New England to Georgia there was intense pressure for a national bill of rights as a condition of ratification. Some federalists at first viewed this as nothing but camouflage for an attempt to frustrate ratification altogether. Alexander Hamilton was angry and contemptuous. It was the plan of the antifederalists, he declared, "to frighten the people with ideal bugbears, in order to mould them to their own purposes. The unceasing cry of these designing croakers is, My friends, your liberty is invaded!" Washington, choosing somewhat milder language, was inclined to agree.

There doubtless was some basis for this opinion; yet it became more and more difficult to hold it unequivocally. Pamphlets and newspaper articles sprouted on both sides of the question, but the antifederalist clamor for a bill of rights clearly had a grass-roots origin. The issue of religious freedom, while not at this time an agitated question, drew some attention. As a committee of Baptist leaders in Virginia saw it, the new Constitution did not make "sufficient provision for the secure enjoyment of religious liberty"; and an imaginative antifederalist writer in Massachusetts complained that although there was no guarantee of freedom of conscience for the people, the ban on religious tests might result in the election of a Mohammedan President.

Concern over individual liberty, of course, was by no means the exclusive property of antifederalists. Indeed, there were many on the other side (including Madison and Jefferson, both of whom must be counted as federalists at this early stage) who were as deeply devoted to liberty as anyone in the antifederalist ranks. Madison had been somewhat wary of a federal bill of rights for fear that specifying what the central government might not infringe would imply that it could suppress other rights, not enumerated. But reconsideration plus advice from Jefferson changed his mind; and numerous other important federalists finally conceded the expedience if not the need of such a bill. The upshot was that as the state conventions one by one ratified the Constitution, most of them did so with a strong recommendation for the addition of protective amendments. Madison found himself, in March of 1789, setting out from Virginia as a representative to the First Congress, pledged to introduce a large batch of amendments. Among them were, in substance, the ten that now make up the Bill of Rights.

With long congressional debates developing over such urgent matters as new revenue laws, and such intriguing ones as whether the Chief Executive should be called "His Highness" or just "the President," it was June before Madison was able to get any action on the proposed amendments. Even then there was some reluctance to discuss a national bill of rights in preference to questions of greater sectional interest, and he was obliged to lecture his House colleagues on what their constituents expected of them—particularly "those safeguards which they have been long accustomed to have interposed between them and the magistrate who exercises the sovereign power." He then presented his list of amendments and gave a long speech defending them. One prophetic point he made was in the form of a quotation from Jefferson saying that the federal courts would "consider themselves in a peculiar manner the guardians of those rights" stipulated in such amendments to the Constitution.

The congressional history of Madison's amendment on religion throws some interesting illumination on the question of just what it meant in its final form, when after much rewording it became part of the First Amendment. He first introduced it as, "The civil rights of none shall be abridged on account of religious belief or worship, nor shall any national religion be established, nor shall the full and equal rights of conscience be in any manner, or on any pretext, abridged." Against the background of the Jefferson-Madison view of religion in its relation to democratic government, the emphasis here is unmistakable. It goes straight to what they conceived to be the heart of the matter: absolute freedom of thought for the individual citizen without government pressure toward any system of belief whatever. It seems likely that, had Madison's original wording been adopted, official sanction for even the vague theism suggested by the motto first engraved on United States coins in 1864 ("In God We Trust"), or by the interpolation in 1954 of "under God" in the national oath of allegiance, would have been considered unconstitutional. (Both resulted from acts of Congress.) Certainly his wording would have buttressed the recent Supreme Court decision against the devotional use of prayers or Bible reading in public schools. Whether it would have thrown light on other controversial church-state issues—for example the payment of chaplains for service in the armed forces—is more problematical.

There is no doubt, however, where Madison and Jefferson stood when it came to practical applications. They were meticulous. In 1789 Madison opposed (unsuccessfully) the appointment of official chaplains for Congress because "these are to be paid out of the national taxes"; and Jefferson, as President, refused to follow the practice of Washington and Adams in proclaiming certain days for religious observance ("I do not believe," he explained, "it is for the interest of religion to invite the civil magistrate to direct its exercises, its discipline, or its doctrines. . . . Fasting and prayer are religious exercises; the enjoining them an act of discipline . . . "). To Madison and Jefferson and their followers the word "establish" meant what it had in Virginia: any government support, by taxation or otherwise, of any religious program.

Madison's original amendment on religion, however, was soon altered. It was referred to a committee of which he was vice-chairman, and evidently caused much discussion—although no exact committee records, unfortunately, were kept. On August 15, 1789, the House as a whole took up the question, considering it in a shorter and less explicit form ("No religion shall be established by law, nor shall the equal rights of conscience be infringed"). Although this wording was less forthright, some members were apprehensive of its effect: Peter Silvester, of New York, said that he "feared it might be thought to have a tendency to abolish religion altogether." The amendment was sent forward to the Senate as, "Congress shall make no law establishing religion, or to prevent the free exercise thereof, or to infringe the rights of conscience." There can be little question that the phrase "or to prevent the free exercise thereof" indicated a desire that the prohibition against establishment should not be interpreted as hostile to religion. The conventional forms of Christianity were still overwhelmingly in use in America, despite significant inroads by deism.

As for Madison, his own sharp focus on utter freedom of thought and expression as the essence of what is now the First Amendment is shown by his introduction, at this time, of an additional amendment specifically forbidding any state to infringe the rights of conscience, freedom of speech, and a free press. This addition was, he thought, "the most valuable on the whole list." Somewhat surprisingly (in view of the antifederalist feeling against domination of the states by the central government), it was sustained by the House, and went to the Senate together with the article on religion and fifteen other amendments.

The twenty-two members of the Senate, which in general was more conservative than the House of Representatives, combined some of the House amendments and dropped others, including Madison's "most valuable" one. Nevertheless, they rejected several motions to amend the House statement on religion to make it prohibit government support of "any particular denomination of religion in preference to another." This was important, for it implied that their intent was to impose a neutral policy on the government with respect to religion in general—not merely to prevent one sect from gaining government favor at the expense of others. Such an intent was suggested further in the rewording arrived at by the Senate on September 9: "Congress shall make no law establishing articles of faith, or a mode of worship, or prohibiting the free exercise of religion." Here the emphasis of "establish" leans toward the idea of government infringement on "the rights of conscience"—even though that phrase was dropped from the House version. The potential application to such matters as public school prayers, for instance, seems obvious.

Yet it was not clear that the Senate's version of the religion clause prohibited tax support, and perhaps for that reason the House refused to accept the revision. A joint committee, with Madison as chairman of the three House members and Oliver Ellsworth of Connecticut as his counterpart for the Senate, then considered the difficulty—again without leaving us minutes of their discussion—and came up with the wording that has become part of the First Amendment: "Congress shall make no law respecting an establishment of religion, or prohibiting the free exercise thereof." Madison could not have been pleased to see the key phrase about "the rights of conscience" abandoned—for him that clarified the basic intent of the amendment—but he was convinced that in its final form the first article of the Bill of Rights could be reasonably interpreted as prohibiting federal support of religious activities in any form.

That, as has been noted, was the way he and Jefferson interpreted it during their terms as President, and for the rest of their lives. At the same time, both of them realized that while they had led a successful campaign for separation of church and state as an essential footing in the structure of democracy, their theoretical reasons for doing so were grasped by relatively few of their countrymen. They knew their ideal was still remote: a society so free that its only ideological commitment would be to freedom of the mind. Much of the support they had been able to rally for a barrier between church and state had other sources. True, it sprang in part from a native intellectual current against absolutism which has never failed to flow in America despite counteracting currents of great force. But in part it came from the mutual and competitive mistrust of the various religious sects toward one another. Always pragmatic, Jefferson and Madison saw the value of this, despite their own rejection of revealed religion. Variety of belief was a useful insurance against tyranny.

The history of the First Amendment since 1791, when the last of the necessary eleven states ratified the federal Bill of Rights, has been one of fluctuating interpretation. This has been most notable during the last fifty years, during which, for the most part, the Supreme Court has found that the Fourteenth Amendment enjoins the guarantees of the First upon the states, for the protection of every citizen. There has been some confusion and inconsistency: schoolchildren swear allegiance to one nation "under God," yet cannot be led in official school prayers, however nondenominational. Over a period of years, however, the trend of Court decisions has been toward strict separation of church and state, in a manner that assuredly would please Jefferson and Madison if they were here to see it. Indeed, the Justices have shown a strong penchant for citing these champions of freedom in explaining and supporting recent Court decisions.

There is nothing sacred about the reasoning of any of our ancestors, on this or any other matter. But whether one agrees with Jefferson and Madison or not, with regard to how high and impassable the wall between church and state ought to stand in a free society, they deserve to be remembered and understood, as the two among the Founding Fathers who devoted more of their minds and lives to this great problem than anyone else. They were an intellectual *avant-garde* whose probing of the relationship between religion and democracy went beyond the more or less traditional attitudes of most Americans between 1776 and 1791. Yet they were the center of a high-pressure area in the climate of opinion of their time, and their conclusions were strongly reflected in the Constitution as it finally was adopted.

Their thinking, moreover, can be fairly understood only as emerging from the matrix of the Enlightenment, of which—with such men as Benjamin Franklin, Thomas Paine, James Monroe, and even George Washington and John Adams— they were indubitably the intellectual offspring. The impact of "natural religion" on the genesis of democratic liberty, through their influence, has too often been ignored.

Writing to Dr. Benjamin Rush in 1800, shortly before he became President, Jefferson alleged certain clerical "schemes" to breach the religion clause of the First Amendment. He would oppose them with all his power, he said, "for I have sworn upon the altar of God eternal hostility against every form of tyranny over the mind of man." It was "Nature's God" that he was thinking of; and for that vow above all others the altar was not to be found, he believed, within the limits of any dogmatic creed.

October 1963

QUESTIONS

1. Examine the assumptions you hold regarding man's nature. Do you share the outlook of the "Founding Fathers" that reason must act to guide behavior? Are there certain absolute moral standards that all people share?

2. Discuss utilitarian philosophy and consider why it often is the basis by which we resolve a moral dilemma.

3. How do we teach moral responsibility? What obligations does "society" have to encourage moral growth?

CHAPTER 2

"THE WALL OF SEPARATION"

Richard B. Morris

For many the search for virtue in everyday life comes up empty. Frustrated by the absence of a religious foundation particularly in the schools, they argue that today's secular humanist culture lacks moral standards. In particular, they point to the abandonment of religion brought about by the separation of church and state. As Richard Morris describes, this "wall of separation" is not strong and sturdy. It is defined by whatever preconceptions individuals have about the First Amendment and our Founding Father's intentions. Morris sets the context for this First Amendment debate telling us that though united on the issue of religious toleration, our Founding Fathers were divided on how to deal with systems of morality and ethics. This essay considers the tradeoff between tolerance and freedom, principles and standards, which play out in a democratic society.

The Supreme Court has been busy of late scrutinizing the "wall of separation," a figure of speech attributed to Thomas Jefferson. It is not like the ugly Berlin Wall, built of concrete blocks and topped with broken glass and barbed wire. Rather it is more like a double-mirrored screen. Persons standing on either side discover whatever preconceptions about the First Amendment they may have brought with them.

And so it was in the Supreme Court decision of March 5, 1984, on *Lynch v. Donnelly*. Standing on one side of the mirrored screen, four men and one woman on the High Court found that the Establishment Clause of the First Amendment—the clause that prohibits Congress from making any law establishing a religion—did not prohibit the city of Pawtucket, Rhode Island, from including a crèche, or nativity scene, in its annual Christmas display. Speaking for the majority, Chief Justice Warren Burger, in overruling the lower court, argued that the crèche, "like a painting, is passive. . . . To forbid the use of this one passive symbol . . . would be a stilted overreaction contrary to our history and to our holdings." The four dissenters looked at the reverse side of the mirror and, with Justice William Brennan as their spokesman, found that Pawtucket had taken "an impermissible step toward the establishment of religion."

The close division on this case by the High Court reflects sharply divided nationwide opinion about the range and limits of the First Amendment, a confusion to which courts in the past have signally contributed in defining the permissible parameters of governmental intrusion in matters of private conscience. Courts have a penchant for probing history to discover the intention of the framers of legislation and amendments. Regrettably they generally find what they are looking for, and their explorations into the past seldom contribute to its enlightenment.

Suppose we ourselves do the probing. Just what does the First Amendment say, what did its author think it said, and finally, how has this very first of the Bill of Rights been faring of late?

The First Amendment, like the rest of the Bill of Rights, was adopted in response to widespread demand on the part of the state conventions that ratified the federal Constitution. These conventions sought to protect civil liberties from the overarching power of a Leviathan state and to make certain substantive changes in the Great Charter as well. The state conventions proposed more than two hundred amendments. James Madison headed a committee delegated by Congress to come up with an acceptable package. He whittled the total down to fourteen (eliminating all that involved substantive changes). After considerable debate Congress narrowed the list still further to twelve. Of these first twelve amendments, two failed to be ratified by the states. The remaining ten (the Bill of Rights) became a part of the Constitution on December 15, 1791.

The relevant portion of the First Amendment, which, with some alterations by others, was Madison's handiwork, reads: "Congress shall make no law respecting an establishment of religion, or prohibiting the free exercise thereof . . . "

Note that the amendment restricts *Congress*, not the states, because, at the time the Bill of Rights was ratified, at least two states, Massachusetts and Connecticut, already had established religions. In other states test oaths barred persons of some religious denominations from voting or holding state office. In a sweeping constitutional revolution initiated in the 1940s by the Supreme Court, the Fourteenth Amendment was construed, some seventy years after it was passed, to extend this prohibition to the states as well as to Congress.

Since the 1940s the Supreme Court has valiantly upheld the prohibition against the establishment of religion while chipping away at its foundations. In taking such opposing positions, the justices have sought to read James Madison's mind. We do know that young Madison had found the persecution of religious dissenters in his area of Virginia abhorrent, "a diabolical, hell-conceived principle." He shared with George Mason and Edmund Randolph in the drafting of Virginia's Declaration of Rights, especially the guarantee of "free exercise of religion." He joined with Thomas Jefferson in moving toward the disestablishment of the Anglican church in Virginia. In the 1780s Madison assumed the principal role in mounting a campaign against Patrick Henry and other prominent advocates of a bill that would assess everyone to pay a tax to the Christian church of the taxpayer's choice. To propagandize his opposition, he wrote a private paper, later printed and widely circulated in 1785 under the title *Memorial and Remonstrance Against Religious Assessments.*

Arguing that religious belief "must be left to the conviction and conscience of every man," he opposed tax support for any and all denominations. However, the reason he advanced was not that of a Deist or an atheist but quite the opposite. He believed that any regulation of religion was "adverse to the diffusion of the light of Christianity," which the *Remonstrance* accepted as the true faith. Madison denounced the bill as an expression of "unchristian timidity." His argument swayed enough votes to defeat the assessment bill.

Although the *Remonstrance* was a private pamphlet, never enacted into law, it was the principal authority, more than 160 years later, for the dissenting opinion of Justice Rutledge in a 1947 decision of the Supreme Court, in which a 5-to-4 majority upheld reimbursing parents with public funds for costs of busing their children to parochial schools. Since then the constitutionality of providing textbooks for parochial schools out of public funds has been upheld, and now the Supreme Court has seen fit to permit the public display of a crèche, a symbol sacred to Christianity. The majority found that the "wall of separation" between church and state is hardly an accurate description of the relationship that in fact exists. The Constitution, so held Chief Justice Burger, does not require a complete separation of church and state; contrariwise, "it affirmatively mandates accommodation, not merely tolerance, of all religions, and forbids hostility toward any." Justice Brennan, speaking for the three other dissenters, found that the crèche was not merely a traditional symbol of Christmas like Santa Claus or reindeer but was a symbol of "an event that lies at the heart of Christian faith" and, as such, was "insulting to those who insist for religious or personal reasons that the story of Christ is in no sense a part of 'history' nor an unavoidable element of our national 'heritage.'"

So contradictory is the historical evidence on whether the First Amendment intended to erect a "wall of separation" between church and state, and if so, just what that meant, that it might be instructive to see just what the Founding Fathers of Revolutionary and constitutional days thought about the subject. Unlike the seventeenth-century Puritans, who agreed that there should be a "consociation" of church and state, quite the opposite of a wall of separation, the Founding Fathers ran the gamut in their beliefs from rationalists or Deists like Thomas Paine and Benjamin Franklin to supporters of orthodox piety exemplified by John Adams and John Jay.

Let us remember that in 1774 the First Continental Congress opened sessions with a prayer. The preacher chosen happened to be the Reverend Jacob Duché, an Anglican clergyman who later turned Tory. But Duché's defection did not deter succeeding Congresses from regularly employing chaplains, except during the administration of Thomas Jefferson. There does not seem to be any record of James Madison ever objecting to a chaplain when he himself sat in Congress or to a chaplain opening Congress with prayer during his own administration.

The issue had once been raised at a critical moment and behind closed doors at the Constitutional Convention in Philadelphia. As a result of intensified debate over the suffrage for the lower house, Benjamin Franklin, a man whose fame does not rest upon his religiosity, urged that a clergyman be invited in to offer prayers at the beginning of each session to allay the prevailing discord. Alexander Hamilton rejoined that the convention could be counted on to transact the business entrusted to its care "without the necessity of calling in foreign aid!" And no chaplain ever entered the barred doors of the convention.

Now just what are we to make of a government that exempts church property from taxes, that started a revolution with daily invocation to God by an ordained clergyman, and that included God in the Declaration of Independence while being scrupulously careful to keep God out of the Constitution! What are we to make of a government that has established a tradition by which each incoming President must take an oath of office on the Bible—and what of the first President's inaugural address, reputedly written by James Madison, which offers "fervent supplications to that Almighty Being who rules over the universe" and asks for His benediction on the people of the United States? That same government has regularly employed chaplains in its armed services, has declared Thanksgiving Day a national holiday, has put God into the pledge of allegiance—and imprints IN GOD WE TRUST on the back of every dollar bill.

Finally, it should be pointed out that some of our learned Founding Fathers, notably Dr. Benjamin Rush, advocated that education be conducted in the Christian way. As for Alexander Hamilton, in his later years the embittered politician proposed the creation of a Christian Constitutional Society (it died aborning)—a notion utterly abhorrent to his chief political foes, Jefferson and Madison.

United though the Founding Fathers stood on the issue of religious toleration, they were divided, if not confused, on whether the federal government was to be viewed as strictly neutral in matters of religion or whether it would encourage systems of morality and ethics drawn from the Judeo-Christian tradition.

And at the same time that the issue of the Christmas symbol is disposed of by a court choked with a backlog of cases, we hear the renewed call for prayer in the schools, a call widely trumpeted by public figures and fundamental religionists alike. In the wake of the Supreme Court's acceptance of Pawtucket's crèche, will this further probing of the First Amendment again intensify divisiveness in the nation?

August 1984

QUESTIONS

1. What are the advantages and the disadvantages of established religion? Give examples. How do Judeo-Christian principles support or contradict American political philosophy?

2. Some argue that puritan morality has always been a deep-seated value of the American political culture. do you agree or disagree? Give examples to support your opinion. Are Americans a religious people?

3. What is wrong with prayer in school? Why not teach morality and virtue in school? Would it make a difference?

CHAPTER 3

"A SCANDALOUS, MALICIOUS AND SEDITIOUS LIBEL"

Thomas J. Fleming

Historically, the government's relationship with the press has been guided by the principle of "no prior restraint." But early in our country's history, press and government relations were more tenuous. This is well described in "A Scandalous, Malicious and Seditious Libel," by Richard Morris. Here Morris explains the case of the People v. Croswell (1803. The case of accused libel occurred in the aftermath of the "Alien and Sedition Acts" passed by the Federalist Congress in 1798. The Alien Act limited freedom of the press by attempting to suppress critics of the government. Fortunately the Alien Acts were short lived. Still concern and debate about press freedom remain. Many express concern about biased news coverage, sources of information, and national security. This article helps examine attitudes toward the press and the media in general. It allows us to consider why press freedom was so important to our Founding Fathers and if there are circumstances when the press should be restrained.

"At a Court of general Sessions of the Peace, holden at Claverack, in and for the county of Columbia, it is presented that Harry Croswell, late of the city of Hudson, in the county of Columbia aforesaid, Printer, being a malicious and seditious man, and of a depraved mind and wicked and diabolical disposition, and also deceitfully, wickedly and maliciously devising, contriving and intending, Thomas Jefferson, Esquire, President of the United States of America, to detract from, scandalize, traduce, and vilify, and to represent him, the said Thomas Jefferson, as unworthy of the confidence, respect and attachment of the People of the said United States, . . . and wickedly and seditiously to disturb the Peace and tranquility as well of the People of the State of New York as of the United States; . . . the said Harry Croswell did on the ninth day of September, in the year of our Lord 1802, with force and arms,

at the said city of Hudson, in the said county of Columbia, wickedly, maliciously and seditiously print and publish and cause and procure to be printed and published, a certain scandalous, malicious and seditious libel, in a certain paper or publication entitled 'The Wasp.' . . . "

All history is a mingling of the great and small, of kings losing kingdoms for want of a horseshoe nail, of presidents assassinated because a guard needed a smoke. But seldom has there been a stranger concatenation of the petty and the magnificent, the comic and the tragic, the trivial and the profound, than in the case of the *People v. Croswell*, in 1803. By an odd blend of good and bad luck, an obscure twenty-four-year-old printer wrote himself into the *Dictionary of American Biography*, established the libel law on which contemporary press freedom still rests, jarred the political security of President Thomas Jefferson, and indirectly helped to involve Alexander Hamilton in his fatal duel with Aaron Burr.

In 1803 the infant American Republic was running a high political fever. The ferocity of the verbal warfare raging between the Federalists, the party created by Alexander Hamilton, and the Democratic-Republicans, led by President Jefferson, has rarely been matched in American politics, even by the diatribes of today's New Left and Ultra Right.

The first fusillades had been fired during Washington's Presidency. The Jeffersonians, with not a little help from the Sage of Monticello himself, had set up journalists such as Philip Freneau and Benjamin Franklin Bache with one mission, to deflate and discredit an administration that was, in Jefferson's view, "galloping fast into monarchy." They soon had the Father of His Country in a state of near apoplexy. "That rascal Freneau," as Washington called him, insisted on sending his scurrilous *National Gazette,* published in Philadelphia, to the President's house even after he had cancelled his subscription. Freneau spent most of his abuse on Hamilton. Bache preferred Washington as a target, calling him "treacherous," "mischievous," "inefficient," and sneering at his "farce of disinterestedness" and his "stately journeyings through the American continent in search of personal incense."

These verbal guerrillas soon had imitators. Among the more savage was William Duane, Bache's successor as editor of the Philadelphia *Aurora.* Washington, he wrote, had "discharged the loathings of a sick mind." Even this was topped by an English newcomer, James T. Callender. In the Richmond *Examiner* he declared that "Mr. Washington has been twice a traitor."

The Federalists, the upholders of upper-class dignity, labored under a difficult handicap in such a war. They soon became afraid, in Washington's words, that "there seems to be no bounds to . . . attempts to destroy all confidence, that the People might, and . . . ought to have, in their government; thereby dissolving it, and producing a disunion of the States." The Alien and Sedition Acts of 1798 were an expression of this fear. Passed by a Federalist

Congress with Washington's public approval, the Alien Act gave President John Adams the power to deport any foreigners he deemed dangerous to public peace. The Sedition Act empowered the federal judiciary to punish anyone convicted of false or malicious writing against the nation, the President, or Congress with a fine of not more than $2,000 and imprisonment for not more than two years.

Federalist judges immediately went to work and soon had indictments against Bache, Duane, Callender, and a dozen other Democratic-Republican editors. The Jeffersonians responded at the state level with the Kentucky and Virginia resolutions of 1798, which declared the Alien and Sedition Acts altogether void and introduced the doctrine of nullification into American constitutional thinking—a seed that would bear ominous fruit in a later era. Up and down the land, Jeffersonian editors bellowed mightily that the Federalists were attempting to erase the First Amendment and destroy the free press.

The Jeffersonian counterattack was beautifully executed: the Federalist judges retreated in disarray and all but abandoned the unpopular prosecutions after a mere ten convictions. The nation roared into the election of 1800 with both sides strenuously exercising their right of free speech. But except for a few slugging editors who sneered at "Massa Jefferson" the slave owner, most of the Federalist propaganda came from pulpits, where clergymen pictured the election of the pro-French and "atheistic" Jefferson as the beginning of a Jacobinical reign of terror against religion. In the print shops the Jeffersonians had the bigger, more vituperative guns. James Callender's pamphlet, *The Prospect Before Us,* slandered Washington and Adams with such recklessness that it achieved an unenviable literary fame. Although Federalist papers theoretically outnumbered the Jeffersonians 103 to 64, most of them maintained a tepid semineutrality that permitted the Democratic-Republicans to run away with public opinion and the election. Defeated John Adams wrote mournfully, "If we had been blessed with common sense, we should not have been overthrown by Philip Freneau, Duane, Callender. . . . A group of foreign liars have discomfited the education, the talents, the virtues, and the property of the country."

But the Federalists were down, not out. Older leaders like John Jay might retire to their estates in dismay, but there were numerous young, vigorous Federalists in the prime of middle life, such as Hamilton and Fisher Ames of Massachusetts, who did not feel it was time for them to abandon politics. They decided Federalism was not dead, it had just been misrepresented, distorted, and smeared without rebuttal. It was time to junk the older Federalist ideas about the vulgarity of appealing to the people through the press. Ames suggested a Latin motto as a guide: *Fas est et ab hoste doceri* ("It is perfectly proper to be taught by one's enemy"). Up and down the Republic, Federalists began founding papers in which, Ames declared, "wit and satire should flash like the electrical fire." At the same time, the paper he helped found, the *New*

England Palladium, would, he predicted, be "fastidiously polite and well-bred. It should whip Jacobins as a gentleman would a chimney sweeper, at arms length, and keeping aloof from his soot."

In New York, Alexander Hamilton soon gathered a group of well-heeled Federalists who put up $10,000 for a daily to be called the *Evening Post* (still in business today, as the *New York Post)*. Its editor, William Coleman, met Alexander Hamilton by night and took down his editorials from the very lips of the great man himself. Throughout the other states, similar papers suddenly blossomed: in Baltimore, for example, the *Republican, or, Anti-Democrat;* in South Carolina, the Charleston *Courier.* In Hudson, New York, another group of Federalists led by Elisha Williams, one of the state's most noted attorneys, backed Ezra Sampson as the editor of the *Balance and Columbian Repository.* As a junior editor Sampson hired twenty-two-year-old Harry Croswell.

Connecticut born, this well-built, dignified young man had studied for a time in the household of Noah Webster, later of dictionary fame and a high Federalist of the old school. (Webster's solution for rampant Jeffersonianism was to raise the voting age to forty-five.) Temperamentally, Harry Croswell was a born Federalist. He was religious, had a natural deference for older, wiser, richer men, and tended to see political developments of the day as a clash between the forces of darkness and light.

Hudson at this time was not the somnolent little river town it is today. In the decade after the Revolution it carried more ships on its registers than the city of New York. Much of western Massachusetts and northern Connecticut used Hudson for a shipping center. One March day in 1802, a reporter counted 2,800 sleighs loaded with goods on Hudson's streets, creating a traffic jam of prodigious dimensions. At the same time with Albany, the state capital, a mere twenty- eight miles upriver, it was hardly surprising that Hudson and surrounding Columbia County were politically sensitive areas. Later in the century one local historian unabashedly claimed that the county had produced more distinguished politicians than any other comparable area in the entire country.

The Jeffersonians were strongly entrenched there. In 1802, the attorney general of the state of New York was sharp-eyed, hatchet-faced Ambrose Spencer, a native son of Columbia County. Morgan Lewis, chief justice of the state supreme court, was married to Gertrude Livingston, whose family's vast upstate holdings included a large chunk of the southern portion of the county. The Livingstons were the most potent voice in the Jeffersonian party at that time.

It was hardly surprising, therefore, that the Jeffersonians decided to set up a rival to the Federalist *Balance.* For their printer they chose Charles Holt, former editor of the New London *Bee* and a Sedition Act martyr who had been convicted in 1800 for libel and spent several months in jail. Holt prepared to launch a *Bee* in Hudson and made it clear it would buzz impertinently in the face of the dignified *Balance.*

Young Harry Croswell forthwith saw an opportunity to prove his extreme devotion to Federalism. He persuaded his senior editor, Sampson, to let him publish in the garret of the *Balance* office a paper entitled the *Wasp.* As an editorial pseudonym, Croswell chose "Robert Rusticoat"; for a motto, "To lash the Rascals naked through the world." Down in New York, an observer in the *Evening Post* told the story in doggerel obviously modelled on "Yankee Doodle."

> *There's Charlie Holt is come to town*
> > *A proper lad with types, sir.*
> *The Democrats have fetched him here*
> > *To give the federals stripes, sir.*
>
> *The Balance-folks seem cruel 'fraid*
> > *That he'll pull down their scales, sir.*
> *And so they got a pokerish wasp,*
> > *To sting hint with his tail, sir.*

Croswell's opening number was nothing less than a declaration of war:

Wherever the Bee ranges, the Wasp will follow over the same fields and on the same flowers—Without attempting to please his friends, the Wasp will only strive to displease, vex and torment his enemies. . . . The Wasp has a dirty and disagreeable job to perform. He has undertaken the chastisement of a set of fellows who are entrenched in filth—who like lazy swine are wallowing in a puddle. He must therefore wade knee deep in smut before he can meet his enemies on their own ground.

At his opposite number, Holt, Croswell levelled the following blast:

It is well known that you was bro't here by virtue of $500 raised for that purpose by the leading Democrats in this city. That the public may know, therefore, with how much purity and independence you will conduct in your editorial labors, would you be kind enough to answer the following questions:

Did the contributors to the $500 purchase you, as they purchase Negroes in Virginia, or hire you as they hire servants in New England?

Are you not a mere automaton in the hands of your masters; pledged to publish whatever slanders or falsehoods they shall dictate? And by your contract with them if you refuse to pollute your sheets have they not a right to ship you back again to your 350 subscribers in New London?

Croswell soon made it clear that this was more than a local war. Down in Virginia, James Callender was demonstrating his lack of principle by turning on his former idol, Thomas Jefferson. After Jefferson became President,

Callender, working on the assumption that his slanderous attack on Washington and Adams had done much to swing the election, coolly asked to be made postmaster of Richmond. Jefferson declined, whereupon Callender revealed in print that while he was working on *The Prospect Before Us,* Jefferson had sent him a hundred dollars and had even read part of the manuscript, returning it with the declaration, "Such papers cannot fail to produce the best affect. They inform the thinking part of the nation . . . "

This was sensational stuff, the kind of thing that could hurt Jefferson politically. Washington was now in his grave two years and already the process of canonization was in full swing. Federalist printers rushed to their presses to discuss Jefferson's rather lame explanation that he had sent Callender the hundred dollars out of charity, and because he was a Sedition Act victim. But few equalled the savagery with which the *Wasp* pilloried this explanation.

> It amounts to this then. He [Jefferson] read the book and from that book inferred that Callender was an object of charity. Why! One who presented a face bloated with vices, a heart black as hell—one who could be guilty of such foul falsehoods, such vile aspersions of the best and greatest man the world has yet known—he an object of charity! No! He is the very man, that an aspiring mean and hollow hypocrite would press into the service of crime. He is precisely qualified to become a tool—to spit the venom and scatter the malicious, poisonous slanders of his employer. He, in short, is the very man that a dissembling patriot, pretended "man of the people" would employ to plunge for him the dagger, or administer the arsenic.

Again and again Croswell sank his stinger into this Jeffersonian blister.

> Will the reader turn to that inaugural speech of 1801 and see how this incarnate (Jefferson) speaks of Washington. There he makes him a demigod—having already paid Callender for making him a devil . . . Will the word hypocrite describe this man? There is not strength enough in the term.

When Holt attempted to answer Croswell by impugning Callender's character, the young Federalist editor hoisted him with another petard.

> About the time of Callender's trial, you [Holt] printed a paper in New London—in that paper Callender was extolled to the skies. He was then an "excellent Republican," a "virtuous man," a "good citizen," a "suffering patriot." . . . If there is anything on earth to be pitied, it is a miser-"able editor" constantly tumbling into the mire; and whose every struggle but sinks him deeper.

The disarray of his antagonists emboldened Croswell to aim some shafts at local Democratic-Republicans. In the September 9, 1802, issue of the *Wasp* appeared the following poem:

> *Th' attorney general chanc'd one day to meet*
> *A dirty, ragged fellow in the street*
> *   A noisy swaggering beast*
> *   With rum half drunk at least*
> *Th' attorney, too, was drunk—but not with grog—*
> *Power and pride had set his head agog.*

The poem went on to describe how the attorney general, "madly frowning on the clown," asked him how he had the insolence to address him as a "fellow lab'rer for the common good."

> *"Why, "" said the fellow with a smile,*
> *"You weekly in the paper toil,*
> *"Condemn the old administration*
> *"And do your best to 'save the nation'*
> *"While I with just the same pretenses*
> *"Chalk 'Damn the Feds' on gates and fences."*

Croswell lampooned other leading local characters who were perfectly recognizable even when he named no names. One satire described a prominent judge who spent an evening eating and drinking at a nearby tavern and then refused to pay his bill. In a memoir that he attached to one of the few surviving complete sets of the *Wasp* (now at the New York Historical Society), Croswell told how he was walking through the streets of Hudson, not long after publication of the latter tale, when up thundered a local justice of the peace, a big man named Hagedorn, who leaped off his wagon, shook his horsewhip under Croswell's nose, and vowed that he considered the tavern story slander and was going to extract instant revenge.

"I had no cane or other means of defense," Croswell wrote. "But I stood erect and dropping my hands to my sides looked him full in the face and in the most cool and collected manner apprised him that . . . neither he nor any other man could ever whip me and it was a mistake for him to talk so loud about it. He . . . broke out again in a tempest of oaths, turned shortly on his heel, mounted his wagon and drove off at a furious pace, his poor horse having received the rash intended for me."

Looking around him, Croswell noticed a staunch Federalist friend in a nearby doorway laughing heartily at the exchange. "Harry Croswell," said he, "how could you be so sure that he would not whip you?"

"Mainly," Croswell replied, "because I planned to run away if he had attempted it."

It never seemed to occur to Croswell that he was a David taking on a number of political Goliaths. One reason may have been the illusion created by the preponderance of Federalists in Hudson. Among his prominent contributors was a young attorney, Thomas Grosvenor, who was the brother-in-law of

Elisha Williams. Williams did more than merely threaten Charlie Holt when the *Bee* turned some of its venom in his direction. He caught the small, thin Holt, described as a "cripple" by a Columbia County antiquarian, and with several supporters nearby, thrashed him thoroughly.

Meanwhile, Croswell broadened his attacks on Jefferson with other choice tidbits from Callender's pen. He quoted the erstwhile Jeffersonian as declaring that "Mr. Jefferson has for years past while his wife was living and does now since she is dead, keep a woolly headed concubine by the name of Sally—that by her he had had several children, and that one by the name of Tom has since his father's election taken upon himself many airs of importance, and boasted his extraction from a President." To this, Croswell added another noxious tale: how Jefferson, before his marriage, attempted to seduce Mrs. John Walker, the wife of a close friend.

Other extremist Federalist papers were printing the same stories. Publicly, Jefferson always maintained a philosopher's stance toward the abuse he was getting. In 1803 he wrote to a European friend, "[It] is so difficult to draw a line of separation between the abuse and the wholesome use of the press, that as yet we have found it better to trust the public judgment, rather than the magistrate, with the discrimination between truth and falsehood." But his actions in 1803 belied that view. One reason may have been that two out of the three stories the Federalists were spreading were uncomfortably close to the truth. The slave concubine would seem to be sheer slander, but three years later Jefferson admitted privately that the Walker story was essentially accurate; and even his most benevolent biographers find it hard to explain away his relations with Callender.

By private letter and personal messenger, in his wonted style, Jefferson passed the word to his state leaders. "[The] press ought to be restored to its credibility if possible," he told Thomas McKean, the governor of Pennsylvania. " . . . I have therefore long thought that a few prosecutions of the most prominent offenders would have a wholesome effect . . . Not a general prosecution, for that would look like persecution: but a selected one." For the already infuriated Jeffersonians in states where Federalists were most impudent, this was what they had been waiting for. Joseph Dennie, the arch-Federalist editor of the Philadelphia *Port Folio,* was promptly charged with seditious libel against the state and the United States. In New York, the selected victim was Harry Croswell.

Several historians have wondered why this obscure editor was singled out rather than the prestigious William Coleman of the *Evening Post,* who had also reprinted Callender's anti-Jefferson blasts. But even a rudimentary sketch of New York politics in 1802 makes it easy to see why Croswell was Attorney General Ambrose Spencer's number-one choice. There is nothing like smiting the enemy when he has had the effrontery to invade one of your most powerful bastions. To underscore this fact, Spencer himself appeared to prosecute the case, with the local district attorney, Ebenezer Foote, serving merely as an assistant.

Spencer was an ex-Federalist who had "gone over" to the other party, and seeing this turncoat undoubtedly made Harry Croswell seethe when he was brought on a bench warrant before three local judges at the Court of General Sessions sitting at Claverack, then the Columbia County seat. The fiery young editor was indicted for libel on two counts, which were duly read to him. One was based on the fourth issue of the *Wasp,* August 12, 1802, in which he had listed "a few 'squally' facts"—five executive acts by President Jefferson which, Croswell maintained, grossly violated the federal Constitution. The second and more serious charge was based on a paragraph that had appeared in the *Wasp* on September 9, 1802:

> Holt says, the burden of the Federal song is, that Mr. Jefferson paid Callender for writing against the late administration. This is wholly false. The charge is explicitly this:— Jefferson paid Callender for calling Washington a traitor, a robber, and a perjurer—. For calling Adams, a hoary headed incendiary; and for most grossly slandering the private characters of men, who, he well knew were virtuous. These charges, not a democratic editor has yet dared, or ever will dare to meet in an open manly discussion.

Croswell was not deserted by his Federalist friends. Standing beside him at the bar were Elisha Williams, Jacob Rutsen Van Rensselaer, and William W. Van Ness. Williams was already established as a legal giant. Oliver Wendell Holmes, in *The Poet at the Breakfast Table,* wrote that he once asked a distinguished New Yorker, "Who on the whole seems the most considerable person you ever met?" Quite to Holmes's bemusement, the man replied without hesitation, "Elisha Williams." Van Rensselaer was a vigorous descendant of the great patron family that had once owned 62,000 acres of land on the east side of the Hudson River, including the entire town of Claverack. Van Ness at twenty-seven was considered the most brilliant young attorney in Columbia County. His folksy courtroom manner was typical of the younger Federalists' new style. He often interrupted his speeches to ask the foreman of the jury for a chew of tobacco.

The tone of the trial was set from the very first defense motion. Croswell's counsel demanded copies of the indictments before entering a plea. The Attorney General objected and was sustained by the all-Republican bench, and Croswell pleaded not guilty. (In his *Wasp* memoir Croswell says that the Jefferson- Callender passage, which was to become the heart of the case, had actually been written by Thomas Grosvenor, but he declined to implicate this young man and took his chances before the court. This required courage. A sojourn in a crude county jail was no laughing matter in 1803.) The defense then requested a postponement until the next session of the circuit court. They argued that on an issue as legally complex as the law of libel, a state supreme court justice should sit. The Attorney General objected; he was promptly upheld.

The defense now made a most significant motion—a request for postponement in order to bring from Virginia James Callender himself, who would testify to the truth of the libel. Attorney General Spencer sprang to his feet, quivering like a wire. Under no circumstances would he tolerate such a procedure. They were trying this case according to the law of New York state. The truth or falsehood of the libel was irrelevant! All he had to prove to the twelve good men and true in the jury box was the question of fact. Did Harry Croswell publish these libelous statements against the President of the United States?

Thus in the small country courtroom before three farmer justices of the peace, the political-legal giants of the Empire State drew historic—and ironic— battle lines. Here was the Jeffersonian attorney general, backed by Jeffersonian justices, vociferously upholding the Royalist doctrine that had been brought to bear against John Peter Zenger at his famous trial in 1735.

But the Zenger case is by no means the landmark in the history of press freedom that has sometimes been supposed. The German printer's acquittal on charges of seditious libel against Governor William Cosby changed very little. The jury had simply disregarded the judge's admonition to disregard the question of the truth of the alleged libel, and the law remained as it was. Subsequent cases in New York and other colonies made it clear that American legislators and most voters were ready to support freedom of the press only when the press printed what they approved.

Essentially, in fact, what colonial and post-Revolutionary liberals meant by freedom of the press was a press free from licensing and prior censorship. When the framers wrote in the First Amendment, "Congress shall make no law . . . abridging the freedom of speech, or of the press," the key word to them was "Congress." The reason Jefferson had considered the Sedition Act null was not because it had muzzled his party's press, but because he was convinced that Congress, under the Constitution, had no power to enact such legislation. Writing to Abigail Adams in 1804, Jefferson would declare, "While we deny that Congress have a right to control the freedom of the press, we have ever asserted the right of the States, and their exclusive right, to do so."

Thus the Jeffersonians were not as inconsistent as they seemed to be in their stand on Harry Croswell. They rooted their opinion in the common-law tradition of England, best summed up by the great commentator Sir William Blackstone:

> The liberty of the press is indeed essential to the nature of a free state; but this consists in laying no previous restraints upon publications and not in freedom from censure for criminal matter when published. Every free man

has an undoubted right to lay what sentiments he pleases before the public; to forbid this is to destroy the freedom of the press; but if he publishes what is improper, mischievous or illegal, he must take the consequences of his own temerity.

But legal principles, even legal traditions, while they may be revered by lawyers and utilized in emergencies like the one in which Ambrose Spencer found himself, are not so sacred to the man in the street, and Croswell's trial soon made it clear that the Jeffersonians were riding a tiger of their own creation. The moment Spencer declared that "the truth cannot be given in evidence," Elisha Williams unlimbered his heaviest rhetorical artillery. Hitherto, he pointed out, it had been the first article in Spencer's political creed that the people possessed the sovereignty and that governors and Presidents were their servants; and that whenever the people should write on their ballots, "Turn them out. Turn them out," those whom they had rejected must fall. But how could this power, this sovereignty, be correctly exercised, how could the people "pluck down the vicious demagogue and raise and support the virtuous patriot unless their variant conduct could be faithfully represented? And what printer would dare to represent such conduct if the truth of the fact so represented could not shield him from destruction?"

Almost immediately Spencer began to backwater. He first agreed to postpone trial of the indictment based an the *Wasp*'s claim that Jefferson had violated the Constitution. But he insisted on taking up the second indictment, the charge in regard to Callender, the next day.

Croswell's attorneys appeared in court the next evening and entered a formal affidavit stating that the Federalists intended and expected to prove the truth of the facts as stated in the *Wasp* in regard to Callender and President Jefferson. Like a shrewd fencer, the Attorney General returned an unexpected riposte. He wanted Croswell bound with $5,000 bail on each indictment "to keep the peace and be of good behavior." Croswell's attorneys exploded in a chorus of objections. Not only was such a demand illegal and a violation of Croswell's liberty as a free citizen of the United States—it was indirectly an attack upon the freedom of the press.

Elisha Williams and his confreres spent most of the next day debating this motion with Spencer. Again the political deficiencies of the Jeffersonian case were evident. Spencer, representative of the party that claimed to be the repository of the true spirit of the American Revolution, spent most of his time quoting cases out of English common law. The principal citation was a statute from the reign of Edward III which granted justices power to bind over "such as be not of good fame" to be of good behavior. Williams came back with a rain of English citations, including the still politically potent name of John Wilkes. When this erratic friend of the American Revolution had been arrested for libel in 1763 and the King's attorney attempted to have him bound, the Chief Justice of England dismissed the motion, "whereupon there was a loud huzzah in Westminster Hall."

The Attorney General rose with a rebuttal that the reporter for the *Balance* grudgingly admitted was, "with the exception of a few indecent expressions . . . one of Mr. Spencer's most ingenious speeches." But in spite of his ingenuity, Spencer's motion to bind Croswell was denied. The Republican judges could not bring themselves to gag Croswell quite so flagrantly.

Six months of legal jousting followed. The Croswell attorneys fought to get the entire case transferred to the circuit court, under a New York supreme court justice, and Spencer struggled to retain it in the lower court, where he would have a local Jeffersonian bench and jury. In the interim, however, the Federalists scored a resounding electoral victory in Hudson and duplicated it in five other Columbia County towns.

The legal battle reached a climax on June 14, 1803, when Spencer and the Croswell legal trio once more clashed at Claverack. After a long and acrimonious debate, Spencer gave way and agreed that both indictments could be tried before a supreme court justice on the next circuit through the county. It soon became evident that Spencer had a good reason for accommodating his opponents. Chief Justice Morgan Lewis appeared as the circuit judge. A thorough Jeffersonian, Lewis interrupted Croswell's lawyers as they once more attempted to request a delay in order to obtain evidence from James Callender in Virginia. Such evidence, Lewis declared, concerned the truth of the charge for which the defendant was indicted and in his opinion the law was "settled, that the truth could not be given in evidence to the jury as a justification."

Croswell's lawyers argued manfully against this prejudgment. They maintained that Croswell's case involved a public libel, which made the truth of vital consideration. On that ground, they requested a delay until a commission appointed by the court could examine Callender. (At this point in his career, Callender was on his way to becoming a hopeless drunkard, and Croswell's lawyers probably felt that he would be a sorry witness at best; hence the shift to a commission to examine him at a distance.)

Judge Lewis was unmoved by the Federalist eloquence. When the Attorney General rose to reply, the Chief Justice told him it was unnecessary. He said he was "astonished" at the application, and repeated his view that "the law is settled, that the truth of the matter published cannot be given in evidence." Then, suggesting the nervous state of the Jeffersonian position, his Honor hastened to add, "I very much regret that the law is not otherwise; but as I am to declare what the law is, I cannot on this ground put off the trial."

The outcome of the trial was easily predictable. The only thing that really mattered was the Chief Justice's charge to the jury, in which he instructed them that they had but one thing to decide: whether Harry Croswell did in fact publish the scurrilous statements in the *Wasp*. It was left to the court to weigh matters of truth or falsehood, and also of malice, in determining the sentence. The jury retired at "sunsetting" with nothing to debate. Nevertheless, they remained out the whole night, and not until eight o'clock the next morning did they come to the bar with a verdict of guilty.

Croswell's attorneys immediately moved for a new trial, arguing that Lewis had misdirected the jury, and reiterating that the truth should be given in evidence. The motion was granted and the case was carried over first to the November term of the New York supreme court, and finally to the January, 1804, term.

In the meantime, both sides regrouped for the climax of the battle. The Federalists sought out their chief intellect, Alexander Hamilton. As early as June 23, 1803, they had persuaded General Philip Schuyler, Hamilton's father-in-law, to write the brilliant former Secretary of the Treasury for help. (In a style that typified the primeval Federalist, the patrician Schuyler described the case as "a libel against that Jefferson, who disgraces not only the place he fills but produces immorality by his pernicious example.") There is some evidence that Hamilton advised Croswell's counsel before the circuit court trial. Now, with the proceedings at stage center, he agreed to appear in person, gratis.

Down in Virginia during the same months, fate put a dent in Croswell's cause. In the midst of a drunken spree his potential star witness, Callender, fell out of a boat to find a final resting place, as one writer put it, "in congenial mud" at the bottom of the James River. But he left behind him his published works, including letters Jefferson had written expressing his approval of *The Prospect Before Us,* so his dirty work was very much alive when the supreme court convened February 13, 1804, to hear the final round of *People v. Croswell.*

For Hamilton the case represented an opportunity for revenge against his great rival, who was riding high on the crest of political triumph. Some of it Jefferson owed to Hamilton, whose unwise attempt to dump John Adams as the Federalist candidate in 1800 had done much to hand Jefferson the election. Aaron Burr had in the same year destroyed Hamilton's political power base in New York, manipulating the votes of the Tammany Society to elect a Jeffersonian governor, George Clinton. Discredited with his own party, Hamilton had retreated to his law practice, where he had already established himself by his sheer brilliance as a thinker and speaker.

More than revenge may have stirred Hamilton in the Croswell case. This strange, often contradictory giant, who was considered by Talleyrand to be one of the three greatest men of the age along with Napoleon and Pitt, had a deep, instinctive love of liberty which was never extinguished by his vision of a compact organic society, organized and run by a natural aristocracy at the top. Now free from the inhibitions and necessities of party intrigue, which had prompted him to approve the Sedition Act, he flung himself wholeheartedly into Croswell's defense.

He brought with him from New York an old friend and staunch Federalist, Richard Harrison, who had shared Hamilton's mind and heart since their days together as Washington's aides-de-camp. With these two lawyers of the first rank was young William Van Ness, to provide continuity from the earlier court battles.

The opposition, meanwhile, had made a notable change. On February 3, 1804, Attorney General Ambrose Spencer had been nominated to the supreme court, but he properly abstained from sitting on the case, and summoned one of his political followers, George Caines, as his associate before the bar. Spencer's abstention left a four-man court: Chief Justice Lewis, who had already proved himself a devout Jeffersonian; Brockholst Livingston, who, true to his family reputation, was of a similar political faith; a third Jeffersonian, Smith Thompson; and a lone Federalist, James Kent.

But in force of personality and weight of learning, Kent more than equalled the three Jeffersonian justices. "The American Blackstone," as he was later called for his *Commentaries on American Law,* the most influential legal volumes of the nineteenth century, had been converted to Federalism by listening to Alexander Hamilton's magnificent speeches in favor of the Constitution during the New York state ratifying convention in 1789, and by the still more cogent reasoning of the *Federalist Papers.* It was from a friendship with Hamilton begun in those days that he had acquired his conviction that the common-law tradition was essential to the nation's future. Not all lawyers agreed with this in 1804. In most states, the best legal minds were debating whether they should not scrap the common law and create a whole new code, as the French had done under Napoleon.

The problems—and the advantages—of the common law were all too evident in Croswell's case. All of the first day of the trial and most of the second were consumed by excursions far back into the mazes of English common law, with both sides endeavoring to show that the legal tradition of an earlier and supposedly purer age upheld their view of the central question: whether the truth could be admitted as evidence in a case of seditious libel. It was something of a stand-off; but it did clear away legal debris and effectively set the stage for Alexander Hamilton.

By now the hearing was absorbing the attention of both the judicial and legislative wings of New York's state government. According to Charles Holt's *Bee,* almost the entire state senate and assembly poured into the supreme court chambers to hear the climax of the debate. They were there for more than the excitement of seeing Hamilton in action. Already a legislator had submitted a bill that would permit the truth to be heard in libel cases. The British Parliament had passed a similar bill in 1792.

No exact record of Hamilton's speeches in the Croswell case exists, but New York papers reported them quite fully and Justice James Kent kept ample notes. Hamilton began by emphasizing the importance of the subject and went on to examine what he called "the two Great Points"—the truth as evidence, and the jury's right to examine Croswell's intent. He insisted he was not arguing for "the pestilential Doctrine of an unchecked Press." The best man on earth (Washington) had had his great character besmirched by such a press. No, he was contending for the right to publish "the truth, with good motives, though the censure light on government or individuals." Above all he wanted to see "the check" on the press deposited not in a permanent body of magistrates, but in an "occasionally and fluctuating Body, the jury." He pointed out that in the American system judges were not as independent from the executive and legislative branches as they were in England. All the more reason, therefore, to anchor freedom of the press in the right of trial by jury.

Hamilton ranged up and down English legal history and even dipped into Roman law and scriptural texts, to prove that the common law had always maintained these rights, until it was corrupted by the Star Chamber courts, which only proved his point—"a permanent body of men without the wholesome check of a jury grows absolute." Then he turned and indirectly defended the Sedition Act, which despite its repressive intent had been directed against slander which could be proved to be "false." He declared that he "gloried in" the fact that the United States had "by act" established this doctrine.

From here Hamilton soared into a long paean to the juror's duties and rights. What if this were a "capital case" and the jury decided that it did not agree with the court's interpretation of the law? Everyone knew that jurors were bound by their oaths, in such a case, to vote according to their convictions. Were he himself a juror, Hamilton declared, he would "die on the rack" before he would "violate his convictions on the altar of power."

Throughout the afternoon, Hamilton all but hypnotized his audience with his dazzling oratory. Kent noted that he was "*sublimely eloquent.*" The court adjourned at 5 P.M., and the next morning Hamilton took up the argument again. Once more he worked his way through an impressive number of citations to bolster his argument, but he soon got to the political meat in his morning's work, a digression that Judge Kent in his notes called "*impassioned & most eloquent,*" on the danger to American liberty, not from provisional armies but from "*dependent* judges, from *selected* juries, from *stifling* the Press & the voices of leaders & Patriots."

"We ought to resist, resist, resist, till we hurl the Demagogues & Tyrants from their imaginary Thrones," he cried. Never was there a libel case where the question of truth was more important. "It ought to be distinctly known," he thundered, "whether Mr. Jefferson be guilty or not of so foul an act as the one charged." This catapulted him into a eulogy of the dead Washington that in Kent's opinion was "never surpassed—never equalled."

Finally, he paid sarcastic tribute to the "other party" and especially to their "strange & unexpected compliments on the *Freedom* of the English nation." But, he reiterated, a country is free only where the people have a representation in the government, and where they have a trial by jury. If America abandoned the principles of the common law, a faction in power could construe the Constitution to make "any political Tenet or any Indiscretion a Crime." Sacrificing and crushing individuals "by the perverted Forms & mask of law" was the "most dangerous & destructive Tyranny."

As the stocky figure of the man whom Talleyrand said had "made the fortune of his country" bowed before the black-robed justices and retired to his seat, James Kent jotted a final note—"I never heard him so great." Thus inspired, Kent wrote a masterful opinion decreeing a new trial for Croswell. The power of his personality and his reasoning persuaded his fellow associate justices, Livingston and Thompson, to abandon their Jeffersonian principles and agree with him—at first. But Chief Justice Lewis, by now running hard for Governor, wrote a contrary opinion of his own. He also paid Justice Livingston a little visit, whereupon Livingston suddenly changed his mind. The court thus divided two and two, and the motion for a new trial was denied.

The prosecution could have moved immediately for a judgment against Croswell, but no such motion was made. The Jeffersonians were already badly clawed by their ride on this legal tiger, and they had no penchant for further gouges. Moreover, the New York senators and assemblymen, having heard Hamilton's eloquence, had set to work on a truth-in-libel bill that was certain to pass; the Chief Justice was upholding a legal principle that was about to be officially invalidated. So the case was simply dropped. Its impact, however, was important: other states would soon follow New York's lead, transforming Harry Croswell's case from a *cause célèbre* into one of the bulwarks of our free press.

Croswell's personal troubles were not yet over. Ambrose Spencer returned to Hudson and brought a new suit against Croswell and his mentor, Sampson, for libel. Sampson settled out of court, but the stubborn Croswell refused to back away from the scathing comments he had made about both Spencer and his henchman, District Attorney Ebenezer Foote, in the farewell issue of the *Wasp,* which had appeared on January 26, 1803. Foote submitted a suit of his own. Spencer recovered $126 in damages; poor Foote, attempting to prove he was not a swindler and a blockhead, was ambushed by a host of witnesses who solemnly vowed they had seen him cheat at cards, among other things. The jury awarded him damages of six cents. This final act of low comedy was gleefully reported in the *Balance.*

Croswell now became senior editor of the *Balance* and continued to do battle in the Federalist cause in Hudson until 1809, when he transferred his paper to Albany. This was a mistake. The Federalists there were in disarray, and his support was meager. Debts piled up; in 1811 a leading Federalist who had loaned him money obtained a judgment against him, and the harassed editor served a short sentence in a debtor's prison. It was one indication of the fatal deficiencies of the Federalists as a party. The "best people" were too interested in lining their own purses to make the sacrifices that a successful political machine demanded.

Totally disgusted, Croswell quit newspapering, took Episcopal orders, and after serving briefly as rector of Christ Church in Hudson, moved to Trinity Church in New Haven. He remained in this post, respected and eventually revered, for the next forty-three years. But he never attended another political meeting, or even exercised his rights as a voter. "His revulsion from Federalism was so entire," said one of his acquaintances after his death, "that in later life his tacit sympathy was evidently with the Democratic party."

Thus exit Harry Croswell. As for Alexander Hamilton, the sequel of the Croswell case was tragedy. During the hearings he had stayed at a friend's house near Albany, and in an evening's conversation, he delivered some scathing denunciations of Vice President Aaron Burr, who was soon to run against Chief Justice Lewis for the governorship of New York. In the course of the election campaign, the friend unwisely quoted Hamilton in a letter that got into the newspapers. Lewis won, finishing Burr politically in New York, and the embittered Vice President challenged Hamilton to a duel. The acclaim he won at Croswell's trial may well have played a part in persuading Hamilton to accept— in spite of his personal detestation of duelling, which had been redoubled by the death of his son Philip in a politically inspired duel two years before. Having regained not a little of the stature he had lost within his party, Hamilton may have been more inclined to risk the morning visit to Weehawken in the hope that it would be another step toward undoing his great rival in the White House, Jefferson. He guessed wrong, and paid for it with his life.

December 1967

QUESTIONS

1. Are there ever occasions when the press should be suppressed? Do people have a right to know? Give examples of when the press behaved in a "responsible" manner.
2. Should the private lives of public figures be subject to media scrutiny? Is it fair to judge an individual on the basis of choices made during his or her youth?
3. Can we separate private from public morality? Are there character faults that can affect someone's conduct as a public official?

CHAPTER 4

"A TUB TO THE WHALE" THE ADOPTION OF THE BILL OF RIGHTS

Kenneth R. Bowling

Americans deeply cherish the civil liberties provided them by the Bill of Rights, the first ten amendments to the Constitution. When the Philadelphia convention concluded its work in the fall of 1787, however, the Constitution did not include such a set of guarantees. Kenneth R. Bowling explains that the addition of the Bill of Rights during the First Congress had as much to do with political necessity as it did with principle. James Madison, the mastermind of the Constitution, believed that adding a bill of rights would be distract anti-federalists from the considerable powers being vested in the national government and that the process would consolidate support for the new Constitution. Madison's political calculations proved correct, says Bowling, but so over the next two centuries did the confidence of Madison and Thomas Jefferson that the Bill of Rights would be vouchsafed by both a vigilant citizenry and an assertive judiciary.

The role of the federal Bill of Rights in American constitutional development has been monumental. This fact would have surprised most of the members of the first federal Congress, the body that reluctantly proposed to the states the amendments later called the Bill of Rights. The Federalist majority considered these amendments an unnecessary political expedient of little constitutional importance, and the time spent on them as wasted.

Although many Antifederalists had made many eloquent statements about the importance of a bill of rights during the ratification campaign, the Antifederal minority in Congress recognized that civil-liberty amendments could be advanced by Federalists as a means to divert attention away from the structural and states' rights amendments that they sought. Without the commitment of James Madison, who drafted the amendments and then, virtually begging, guided them, through the House of Representatives, there would have been no federal Bill of Rights in 1791. Although Madison believed bills of rights important for the protection of civil liberties, he led the fight for practical political reasons. But Madison was not a cynic, and historians who allude to his use of the phrase "nauseous project" to describe the process of getting amendments through the Congress quote the Virginian out of context.

Madison was joking to a friend who had sent him a fable, entitled "The Wise Cooks and Foolish Guests," that told the story of how a delicious soup was made by eleven cooks (the ratifying states) was ruined when the guests insisted on various changes in the recipe.

In an anonymous attack on Madison, published while the Virginian led the floor fight for amendments, Noah Webster, although not a member of Congress, expressed the point of view of many of its Federalist members: "It seems to be agreed on all hands that paper declarations of rights are trifling things and no real security to liberty. In general they are a subject of ridicule." The nation regretted that "Congress should spend their time in throwing out an empty tub to catch people" and that "Madison's talents should be employed to bring forward amendments" which "can have little effect upon the merits of the constitution."

Webster's reference to the empty tub was a widely recognized literary allusion. In 1704 Jonathon Swift had written in Tale of a Tub that "seamen have a custom, when they meet a whale, to fling him out an empty tub by way of amusement, to divert him from laying violent hands upon the ship." Both Federalists and Antifederalists on occasion referred to Madison's proposals as "a tub to the whale," that is, insignificant amendments designed to divert attention away from more substantive amendments that would seriously weaken the powers of the federal government or alter the federal-state relationship.

An ambiguity in the meaning of the word amendment arose at the start of the ratification debate and continued throughout the contests. Support for amendments could indicate a desire either that personal liberties be protected or that fundamental changes be made in the balance of power between the state and federal governments and in the structure of the federal government, or both. In this essay I use amendment to refer to both types of proposals and alteration and bill of rights to distinguish between them. Alterations formed a clear majority of the amendments proposed by the states during the ratification process.

Electing the First Federal Congress

By the end of July 1788 eleven states had ratified the Constitution, but Madison and other leaders in the fight to strengthen the federal government during the 1780's had little time for celebration. Their critical, almost fatal, error at the federal Convention- the refusal to attach a bill of rights to the proposed Constitution- had cost dearly, most dramatically when New York Federalists were forced to join the dominant Antifederal majority in their state convention in an official call for a second federal convention, and when North Carolina refused to ratify without prior amendments.

August and September 1788 provided new threats: a group of New Yorkers attempted to unite Antifederalists up and down the coast; Congress deadlocked over where the first federal Congress should meet; and Pennsylvania Antifederalists called the first statewide political party convention in American history for the purpose of proposing amendments and selecting a slate of candidates to support them in the first House of Representatives. Federalists began to fear that Antifederalists might take control of the first Congress. George Washington lamented to Madison that "to be shipwrecked in sight of the port would be the severest of all possible aggravations to our misery."

Aside from the matter of amendments, no national issues arose during the first congressional election in the winter of 1788-89. Antifederalists did not fare well despite Federalist fears. Because of a general willingness on the part of most Antifederalists to give the new system a trial, an expectation of rights-related amendments, and partisan election laws in some states, voters elected six Federalists for every single Antifederalist.

The major contest- and the only one with national coverage- occurred in the Virginia Piedmont during January and February 1789. There, James Madison ran against his friend James Monroe, a moderate Antifederalist. Virginia's Fifth Congressional District had been carefully constructed by Patrick Henry to keep the nationally known and respected Madison out of the House of Representatives. Monroe advocated amendments to a sympathetic constituency, which had been led to believe that Madison was "dogmatically attached to the Constitution in every clause, syllable and letter." Such an opinion about Madison had a firm foundation, but it failed to acknowledge a shift that had gradually taken place in his thinking since he had characterized the subsequent amendments proposed by Massachusetts as a "blemish" and had convincingly argued in the Virginia ratifying convention against a federal bill of rights. Even as late as August 1788 he still desired a trial period of a few years to demonstrate what amendments the Constitution needed. North Carolina's refusal to ratify without amendments and the Antifederalists resurgence as the autumn of 1788 approached converted Madison. It had taken him a year to accept the reality of the drastic mistake, which had been made at the federal Convention.

In private letters that he hoped would be published, Madison stressed that with the Constitution safely ratified, amendments could be considered. Specifically, he favored the proposal of amendments by Congress, rather than "essential rights." "In a number of other particulars," he wrote, "alterations are eligible either on their own account, or on account of those who wish for them." While clearly refuting the allegation that he opposed any amendments, his statement left vague how many and which alterations he would support.

In the balloting for representative, Madison defeated Monroe by a vote of 1,308 to 972. The fact that he had given his word during the campaign underlies all the reasons he later gave for supporting amendments. Virginia Antifederalists questioned the sincerity of Madison's conversion. George Mason emphasized that Madison would never have been elected without making some promises and noted that he had now become "the ostensible patron of amendments. Perhaps some milk and water propositions may be made…by way of throwing out a Tub to the Whale; but of important and substantial Amendments, I have not the least hope."

Madison's Unpopular Quest in Congress

When the first federal Congress assembled, Madison expected no great difficulty in getting the Federalist Congress to propose amendments to the states. On May 4 he have notice that he would offer several in three weeks. He then agreed to two postponements to allow the revenue debate to proceed. Finally, informing his colleagues that he felt bound by honor and duty, on June 8 Madison moved that the House sit as a committee of the whole to receive and debate his proposals. But his colleagues quickly let him know that they did not consider the matter with equal urgency. They were not expressing opposition to the protection of civil liberties; on the contrary, almost all- even Madison's most vocal critics- held advanced libertarian ideas for their times. They had other reasons for opposing the debate. Amendments meant not only protection for civil liberty but potential alterations as well, and these would engender renewed debate over states' rights. In addition, members feared a public display of the deep sectional divisions within the young republic. Most Federalists, basking in their election victory, believed amendments unnecessary either as political stratagem or as protection for personal rights. Federalists called for postponement to allow a trial period for the new system. As Connecticut representative Roger Sherman, one of the most vocal opponents of amendments, expressed it, if the people had really wanted amendments they would have secured them prior to ratification. Antifederalists wanted postponement also, because they suggested Madison's proposals would fall far short of the alterations they sought.

In response to this lack of support, Madison delivered a long speech defending his motives and arguing for the expediency of amendments. Every motive of prudence argued for them, he pleaded; large numbers of Antifederalists would thereafter support the Constitution, and North Carolina and Rhode Island would rejoin the Union. He refused to support structural alterations on the grounds that while some respectable characters had sought them, the mass of the people had been concerned only about encroachments on their liberties. In conclusion, he offered and discussed each one of his proposals. Relying heavily on the Virginia convention's proposed bill of rights, and therefore on George Mason's Virginia Declaration of Rights of 1776, Madison incorporated into his June 8 proposals most of the rights-related amendments recommended by the states. Of the proposed alterations, Madison included only a handful, some of which were considered rights-related as well. In sending off copies of his amendments to correspondents in Virginia and North Carolina, Madison insisted that he had designed them to touch "the structure and stamina of the government" as little as possible. Yet they were "important in the eyes of many and can be objectionable in the eyes of none."

Madison's long and comprehensive speech converted neither the Federalist nor Antifederalist. Madison had "done his duty," South Carolina's Federalist William L. Smith smugly told the house, "and if he did not succeed, he was not to blame." Antifederalists again urged a postponement until the new government had been organized and the House could take up all the amendments of the states. The respect that many members felt for Madison, who acted as a sort of prime minister during the first session of Congress, resulted in the House referring his proposals to the committee as a whole.

Just before Madison made his proposals, Federalist representative George Clymer of Philadelphia speculated on whether Madison meant "merely a tub to the whale, a declaration about the press, liberty of conscience &c. or will suffer himself to be so far frightened with the antifederalism of his own state as to attempt to lop off essentials." After the speech Clymer summed up the view of almost everyone: Madison "has proved a tub" on amendments. Other Federalist representatives characterized Madison's proposals as innocent, nugatory, premature, and unnecessary. Boston's congressman, Fisher Ames, suggested they "may do some good towards quieting men, who attend to sounds only, and may get the mover some popularity which he wishes." Theodore Sedgwick of western Massachusetts thought the introduction of the "water gruel" proposals unwise and of no value politically. On and off the floor of Congress, both Ames and Sedgwick questioned Madison's motives and declared bills of rights to be of no constitutional importance.

Madison received a great deal of reaction to his proposals. "I like it as far as it goes; but I should have been for going further," wrote his mentor Jefferson. Others were less gentle. But letter also brought news he hoped to hear. Federalists and Antifederalists at both Philadelphia and Richmond approved. The news from North Carolina particularly encouraged him. Federalist Samuel Johnston, soon to be elected to the United States Senate, thought "a little flourish and dressing without injuring the substantial part or adding much to its intrinsic value, such as a pompous Declaration of Rights" might be enough to obtain ratification at the state's upcoming second convention.

Six weeks later, on July 21, Madison "begged" the House to take up his proposals. It spent the day debating whether to free the committee of the whole from its assignment and to appoint a select committee instead. Federalists could see no good purpose in discussing the subject below crowded public galleries, and so they established a select committee composed of a member from each state, despite the Antifederalist call for a public debate. The committee, a majority of which was unsympathetic to amendments, reported back to the House a week later. It retained Madison's plan of incorporating the amendments into the body of the Constitution itself, rather than appending them to the document as committee member Roger Sherman urged.

The select committee tightened Madison's prose, rearranged his proposals, and considerably narrowed the absolute guarantees of religious freedom and the equal rights of conscience. Most prominently, the committee gutted the majestic natural-rights preamble, cutting out its declaration of the right of people to reform or change their government whenever it was found adverse or inadequate. Madison had proposed to include a statement concerning the purposes of government- the enjoyment of life and liberty, the acquisition and use of property, and the *pursuit and obtaining of happiness and safety*; but the committee eliminated this language. However, Sherman's attempt to limit Madison's absolute guarantee of the freedoms of speech and press by requiring that the words be decent failed in the committee. Madison, firmly attached to his own ideas if not to his own words, showed displeasure with the revision, although he admitted that perhaps some things had been changed for the better. Sherman thought the committee's proposals probably "harmless and satisfactory to those who are fond of Bills of rights." South Carolina congressman William L. Smith found them inoffensive and perhaps of some strategic benefit.

On August 13 the House debated whether to refer the select committee's report to the committee of the whole. Once again representatives from both parties urged postponement, but the House eventually yielded to Madison. The first motion set off a long debate as Roger Sherman again attempted without success to place any amendments at the end of the Constitution, rather than to incorporate them within the existing text.

From August 13 to 18 the committee of the whole considered each amendment individually. The high point of the debate took place on August 15, a sweltering Saturday, during an exchange between Federalists and Antifederalists. Led by Elbridge Gerry of Massachusetts, the other Antifederal speakers that day were South Carolinians Aedanus Burke, Thomas Tudor Tucker, and Thomas Sumter. Burke declared that the proposals before the amendments were "frothy and full of wind, formed only to please the palate; or they are like a tub thrown out to a whale, to secure the freight of the ship and its peaceful voyage." Madison responded to the attack. Had not Antifederalists told the people that they should oppose the Constitution until they secured these very rights? Had not the amendments he proposed been the ones most strenuously advocated by Antifederal leaders? Who was deceiving whom? He implied. Smith characterized the day's debate as more ill humored and rude than any other that had occurred in Congress.

Two more days of heated debate followed, during which there occurred the first known challenge to a duel among members of Congress. Speaker of the House Frederick A. Muhlenberg of Pennsylvania described the August 18 debate as the most heated and disorderly of the session to that point. At its close, the committee of the whole submitted the select committee's report to the House with only minor changes. Apparently none of the amendments had received the two-thirds majority needed to gain approval by the full House. Somehow Madison needed to garner more votes. President Washington, who had suggested in his inaugural address that Congress propose amendments promoting the rights of freemen without altering the system, provided Madison with written support. The president thought some of Madison's proposals unimportant, but "not foreseeing any evil consequences that can result from their adoption, they have my wishes for a favorable reception in both houses." Lukewarm though it might seem, the note probably influenced House Federalists to unite behind Madison's amendments. In addition, postponement or defeat of them at that stage of the process might provide Antifederalists with new ammunition by which to conduct a campaign for a second convention.

In securing Federalist votes to obtain the necessary two-thirds majority, Madison paid a two-part price: the House voted out the little that remained of his preamble, and it agreed to Sherman's motion that the amendments be placed at the end of the Constitution. Madison feared that this placement would lead to ambiguities about how far the original Constitution had been superseded by the amendments. Actually the change set a precedent for isolating amendments, broadened their role in constitutional law, and made it possible to point to a body of amendments known as the Bill of Rights. It is ironic that credit for this development belongs to a leading opponent of the Bill of Rights, Roger Sherman.

The House made only minor changes in substance to Madison's proposals. Antifederal strategy remained what it had been in the committee of the whole: attempt to get the House to consider all of the amendments of the states and propose specific popular structural alterations. As the debate drew to a close, Burke proposed the power of Congress to regulate federal elections in the states (Article 1, section 4) be circumscribed. Benjamin Goodhue of Massachusetts argued against Burke, reminding his colleagues that "there appeared a large majority against the amendments, when the subject was first introduced, and he has no doubt but that majority still existed." Gerry proposed to add the word *expressly* to what became the Tenth Amendment so that the phrase would read "The powers not expressly delegated by this Constitution... are reserved to the states." Such a change would have dramatically reduced congressional power under the necessary and proper clause (Article 1, section8, paragraph 18).

Although the effort failed, it had the support of William L. Smith, who believed the change would go a long way toward protecting the institution of slavery.

Tucker proposed an alteration forbidding Congress from imposing direct taxes except when duties, imports, and excises proved insufficient and then only after a state had refused to pay a congressional requisition. Federalists, Madison included, saw the elimination of Congress's power to lay direct taxes as the chief Antifederal goal. Samuel Livermore of New Hampshire (besides William Floyd of New York, the only Federalist voting consistently with the Antifederalists) declared it to be the most important amendment to come before the House. "Unless something more effectual was done to improve the Constitution, he knew his constituents would be dissatisfied. As to the amendments already agreed to, they would not value them more than a pinch of snuff; they went to secure the rights never in danger." With the failure of the direct taxation motion, House Antifederalists gave up their futile attempt to attach alterations to the Constitution. Irritated nonetheless, Madison noted privately that Antifederalists had tried to defeat "a plan short of their wishes, but likely to satisfy a great part of their companions in opposition." The last eight days had been "extremely difficult and fatiguing" and "exceedingly wearisome," he complained.

On August 24 the House transmitted seventeen amendments to the Senate. The two Philadelphia representatives, George Clymer and Thomas Fitzsimons, advised their fellow townsman Senator Robert Morris that the Senate should "adopt the whole of them by lump as containing neither good or harm being perfectly innocent." Morris, who believed that the House had wasted valuable time on amendments and held Madison responsible, refused, and reportedly not only treated them contemptuously upon their arrival in the Senate but also joined several colleagues in an attempt at postponement until the next session. At the end of the Senate debate, he concluded that the amendments were merely a tub to the whale, while Senator Pierce Butler of South Carolina referred to them as *milk and water* propositions.

Virginia's two Antifederalist senators, Richard Henry Lee and William Grayson, faced insurmountable odds as they attempted to preserve and strengthen the House proposals. Complaining that Madison's amendments dealt with personal liberty alone, Grayson felt that Madison hoped to break the spirit of the Antifederal party by dividing it. Lee reported a debate over whether liberty of speech and freedom of the press should be struck from the amendments on the grounds that they tended only to encourage licentiousness among the people. One by one the Virginia senators vainly proposed the structural alterations recommended by their ratifying convention but ignored by Madison.

When the Senate completed work on the amendments on September 14, it had made twenty-six changes in the House proposals. In addition to tightening language, it had rearranged and compressed the seventeen articles into twelve and made significant changes in content. Struck from the House list were amendments forbidding the states from infringing upon certain rights of Americans, asserting separation of powers as a principle of the United States government, guaranteeing freedom of conscience, and exempting from military service those with religious objections. Also, the Senate weakened the guarantees of the religious liberty clause. Lee observed to Patrick Henry that the whole idea of subsequent rather than prior amendments to the Constitution had been little better than committing suicide, and Grayson reported to Henry that the proposed amendments were good for nothing and would do more harm than good.

Angered by the Senate changes, Madison reportedly declared that the amendments had lost their sedative virtue and that no amendments at all were better than those adopted by the Senate. Sherman and several congressmen who had reluctantly supported Madison welcomed the Senate's amending hand; consequently, when President Washington forwarded the twelve amendments to the states on October 2, most of the Senate changes remained. Would they satisfy Antifederalists as Madison hoped, or would there be demands by state legislatures for some or all of the additional amendments that the ratification conventions had proposed in 1788 and which Antifederalists had failed to secure in the first Congress in 1789? If there were such demands, they might lead additional states to join Virginia and New York in petitioning Congress to call another constitutional convention.

A Quiet Ratification

Given the intensity of the congressional debate and all the public interest, which the question of amending the Constitution had raised during the campaign to ratify it and during the first congressional election, one would expect great contention over the ratification of Congress' twelve amendments. However, such controversy did not erupt for several reasons. First, Madison's political strategy proved successful. He won support for the Constitution from many Antifederalists who were not particularly concerned about the structural and states' rights amendments that their leaders sought. It had been a brilliant political move, perhaps the most important and successful in his career. As Thomas Jefferson expressed it to the Marquis de Lafayette in April 1790, "the opposition to our new constitution has almost totally disappeared. Some few indeed had gone such lengths in their declarations of hostility that they feel it awkward perhaps to come over, but the amendments proposed by Congress have brought over almost all their followers."

A second reason for the absence of a debate over the ratification of the Bill of Rights related to the concept of federalism, the issue that had been central to American politics for twenty-five years. In implementing the Constitution, the first federal Congress refocused the debate over federalism in a fundamental way. The coalition that had supported a stronger federal government and secured ratification of the Constitution in 1788 achieved stunning legislative successes in the first session of the new Congress. Having attained its major goals and saved the ship of state from the Antifederal whale, the Federalist consensus split along sectional lines. Many Federalists began to move away from their earlier commitment to strengthening the federal government to a position that asserted the importance of protecting the rights of the states. James Madison, who in 1789 had blocked amendments designed to protect states' rights, quickly assumed for himself leadership of their cause in the early national era that lay ahead.

Even before Congress completed its work on the amendments, Antifederalists launched a campaign to stimulate opposition. Samuel Bryan, the most vociferous Pennsylvania Antifederal essayist during the ratification debate, revived his famous "Centinel" series, insisting that Madison's proposals preserved the principle avenues of despotic power for the federal government. He concluded with a call for real amendments, but no one else raised the banner. A flurry of newspaper articles in New York and Philadelphia at the end of 1789 suggested that there would be a public debate on the amendments. Newspapers elsewhere, however, ignored the discussion, apparently following the lead of a widely reprinted article in the *Gazette of the United States* which claimed that the amendments seemed to meet the approbation of the state legislatures; if these amendments did not meet Antifederalists' demands in every respect, the article pointed out, they were nevertheless a concession by Federalists who hoped to reconcile the opposition.

By the end of January 1790 four states had ratified without the question of additional amendments arising. New Jersey was the first. On November 20,1789, it approved all except the second (which provided that no law varying the compensation of members of Congress would be effective until after an ensuing election). Georgia's legislature rejected all twelve on December 1 on the grounds that it was premature to consider amendments when only experience would point out the defective parts of the Constitution. Maryland ratified all twelve on December 19, and New Hampshire approved all but the second on January 25. Three days later Delaware ratified all but the first amendment (which altered the apportionment of the House of Representatives).

On the other hand, by the end of January 1790 two states had called for additional amendments. A month after ratifying the Constitution in November 1789, North Carolina ratified the amendments in their entirety; however, the ratifying convention instructed its future congressional delegation to obtain eight additional amendments, which the convention transmitted to all of the states. South Carolina ratified all of the amendments on January 19, 1790, but at the same time instructed its delegation to secure adoption of the amendments proposed by the state's ratification convention in May 1788.

New York took up the amendments next. Trouble might have been expected from this decidedly Antifederal state. Indeed, had it followed the lead of the Carolinas, the history of the ratification of the Bill of Rights might have been more exciting, for Massachusetts was considering the amendments at the same time and two other key states, Pennsylvania and Virginia, had not yet reached a final decision. But New York did not follow the Carolinas, for Federalists had won control of the state Senate and narrowed Antifederal control of the House in 1789. Despite the fact that leading New York Antifederalists privately declared the amendments to be trivial and equivocal, the state adopted all but the second amendment on February 27.

In January 1790 John Hancock, the Antifederal governor of Massachusetts, transmitted the amendments to the legislature, calling their ratification very important. A month later the two houses agreed to nine of the proposals, rejecting the first two (on apportionment and congressional salaries) and what became the tenth (on the reservation of powers). A joint committee was appointed to bring in a bill, but it never reported, and thus the ratification process was left incomplete in Massachusetts. At the same time, the legislature appointed another joint committee which recommended twelve additional amendments: these, the committee stated, were for the purpose of preserving the forms of a federal republic, and thus preventing a consolidation of the states into one government or the encroachment on the states by the federal government. Although not adopted by the legislature, these proposals created a stir among Federalists throughout the United States, who saw the Massachusetts effort as an attempt to bolster Antifederalists in Rhode Island, the only state that had not yet ratified the Constitution. Federalists also believed that the proposals were designed to weaken the federal government while at the same time launching an opposition to it. The effort failed because the Constitution had much greater popular support in Massachusetts in 1790 than it had had in 1788.

On March 10, 1790, Pennsylvania accepted all but the first and second amendments. In May 1790 the Connecticut General Assembly agreed to all except the first two amendments, but a dispute between the two houses over the procedure prevented final action on any of the amendments. On June 11, 1790, the Rhode Island General Assembly approved all but the congressional-salary amendment. Two weeks earlier, in finally ratifying the Constitution, Rhode Island had proposed twenty-one additional amendments (most of them structural) and listed eighteen rights (drawn from New York's ratification document) that its act of ratification did not compromise or surrender. The additional amendments included several novel ideas, among them a federal guarantee of state sovereignty; a requirement that eleven of the original thirteen states must agree to any amendments after 1793; a provision for an all-volunteer army except in cases of invasion; grants of power to Congress to immediately prevent the importation of slaves and to regulate the "inhabitancy or settlement" of the poor throughout the United States; and a requirement for a two-thirds vote in each house to declare war.

By the end of the second session of the first Congress in 1790, twelve of the thirteen states had acted. Nine had ratified at least ten of the twelve amendments, Georgia had rejected all of them, and Massachusetts and Connecticut had failed to complete the adoption process. With ratification by ten states necessary to adopt the amendments, only one more approval was needed for the amendments to become part of the Constitution.

Virginia was the last state to act. More is known about the two-year ratification process there than in all the other states combined. In late September 1789 the state's Antifederal senators transmitted copies of the proposed amendments to the governor and speaker of the House of Delegates with remarkable covering letters. Expressing their grief, Lee and Grayson declared that they had done all they could do to procure the adoption of the "Radical" amendments proposed by the Virginia ratifying convention. They feared that the Constitution, if not further amended, would produce a consolidated empire, that is, one in which the states were either abolished or ignored. They predicted that if Congress did not propose further amendments, in a few years a sufficient number of state legislatures would demand a second federal convention, unless, of course, "a dangerous apathy should invade the public mind."

Not apathy, as Lee and Grayson feared, but satisfaction with Madison's proposals was what had seized the public mind in Virginia. Federalists reported that the senators' letters were not well received, even by some of the men who had voted against the Constitution at the ratifying convention. Although supported by Patrick Henry, the most powerful remaining Antifederal voice in the United States, a movement to postpone consideration of the amendments until 1790 failed. With defeat looming, Henry abandoned the fray and left Richmond for home. This proved unfortunate for Antifederalists, for at the end of the session a motion to ask Congress to adopt the rest of the Virginia convention's amendments failed by one vote when the speaker was called on to break a tie.

The most respected Antifederalist in Virginia, and perhaps in the nation, was George Mason, whose call for a bill of rights during the ratification process had been so influential. But Mason had been publicly silenced; not only was he an advocate of the rights-related amendments that Congress had proposed, but the very language of these additions had descended verbatim from his 1776 Virginia Declaration of Rights. Privately, however, he had something to say. "Unless some material amendments shall take place," Mason wrote his friend Secretary of State Thomas Jefferson, "I have always apprehended great Danger to the Rights and Liberty of our Country, and to that Cause, in Support of which I have so often had the Honour of acting in Concert with you, I fear in vain!" Jefferson responded that although he approved of the new government on the whole, he too wished to see additional amendments which would fix the federal government "more surely on a republican basis."

In November 1789 a solid majority of the Virginia House of Delegates voted to ratify all twelve amendments. The delegates also appointed a committee to apply to Congress for additional amendments, expressing particular concern about an amendment limiting Congress's power over direct taxation. The state Senate split between those who wanted to adopt and those who feared adoption would kill any chance for additional amendments, particularly one on direct taxation. Its compromise- adopt some and postpone others- was unacceptable to the House, and consequently none of the amendments were adopted.

Both the majority and the minority in the Senate felt compelled to defend their positions in the published journal. The majority's statement was the boldest attempt made by Antifederalists anywhere to use the issue of amendments to stir up opposition to the federal government; but like the Lee and Grayson letters, it failed. The statement condemned the proposed amendments:

> These propositions contain all that Congress are disposed to grant...and that these are offered in full satisfaction of the whole...Considering therefore that they are far short of what the people of Virginia wish, and have asked, and deeming them by no means sufficient to secure the rights of the people, or to render the government safe and desirable, we think our countrymen ought not to be put off with amendments so inadequate.

By June 1790 Richard Henry Lee had reversed himself and come out in favor of ratification. As he told Patrick Henry, no prospect of additional amendments existed during the second session of Congress, but the ones proposed were a beginning that alerted the people to their rights. More could be done later. Lee's final effort was an official letter to the governor in August 1790 calling for Virginia's ratification of the proposed amendments. Despite Senator Lee's appeals, the Virginia legislature did not act immediately. When it did take up the amendments in the fall of 1791, the debate occurred without the previous rancor. On December 15 Virginia completed the adoption of all twelve amendments.

Because Virginia's vote put ten amendments into effect, December 15 is now celebrated as Bill of Rights Day. Nevertheless, to complete the story of the ratification of the Bill of Rights, a few other significant dates should be noted. By the time Virginia acted, the number of states required to adopt the amendments had risen to eleven because Vermont had entered the Union.

CHAPTER 5

REFLECTIONS ON THE BICENTENNIAL OF THE UNITED STATES CONSTITUTION

Thurgood Marshall

In this article regarding the bicentennial of the United States Constitution, the late Supreme Court Justice Thurgood Marshall provides a stark and insightful critique of the original document. We often romanticize the genius of the Framers, Marshall says, but in fact the document they produced was dramatically flawed. The Constitution embraced the institution of slavery as part of a grand political compromise. "We the People" of the Constitution's vaunted preamble was thus a very exclusive club consisting of white property-owning males of at least twenty-one years of age. The Constitution deserving of great praise and celebration, contends Marshall, is the one that exists today as a result of the Reconstruction amendments and other changes that came after the Civil War. The credit for those changes, Marshall maintains, belongs not to the Framers, but to those who came later, and miracle of the Constitution was not its birth but its development over two centuries into a document that safeguards true notions of liberty, justice, and equality.

The year 1987 marks the 200th anniversary of the United States Constitution. A Commission has been established to coordinate the celebration. The official meetings, essay contests, and festivities have begun.

The planned commemoration will span three years, and I am told 1987 is "dedicated to the memory of the Founders and the document they drafted in Philadelphia." We are to "recall the achievements of our Founders and the knowledge and experience that inspired them, the nature of the government they established, its origins, its character, and its ends, and the rights and privileges of citizenship, as well as its attendant responsibilities."

Like many anniversary celebrations, the plan for 1987 takes particular events and holds them up as the source of all the very best that has followed. Patriotic feelings will surely swell, prompting proud proclamations of wisdom, foresight, and sense of justice shared by the framers and reflected in a written document now yellowed with age. This is unfortunate- not the patriotism itself, but the tendency for the celebration to oversimplify, and overlook the many other events that have been instrumental to our achievements as a nation. The focus of this celebration invites a complacent belief that the vision of those who debated and compromised in Philadelphia yielded the "more perfect Union" it is said we now enjoy.

I cannot accept this invitation, for I do not believe that the meaning of the Constitution was forever "fixed" at the Philadelphia Convention. Nor do I find the wisdom, foresight, and sense of justice exhibited by the framers particularly profound. To the contrary, the government they devised was defective from the start, requiring several amendments, a civil war, and momentous social transformation to attain the system of constitutional government, and its respect for the individual freedoms and human rights, that we hold as fundamental today. When contemporary Americans cite "The Constitution," they invoke a concept that is vastly different from what the framers barely began to construct two centuries ago.

For a sense of the evolving nature of the Constitution we need look no further than the first three words of the document's preamble: "We the People." When the Founding Fathers used this phrase in 1787, they did not have in mind the majority of America's citizens. "We the People" included, in the words of the framers, "the whole number of free persons." On a matter so basic as the right to vote, for example, Negro slaves were excluded, although they were counted for representational purposes- at three-fifths each. Women did not gain the right to vote for over a hundred and thirty years.

These omissions were intentional. The records of the framers' debates on the slave question is especially clear: the Southern states acceded to the demands of the New England states for giving Congress broad power to regulate commerce, in exchange for the right to continue the slave trade. The economic interests of the regions coalesced: New Englanders engaged in the "carrying trade" would profit from transporting slaves from Africa as well as goods produced in America by slave labor. The perpetuation of slavery ensured the primary source of wealth in the Southern states.

Despite this clear understanding of the role slavery would play in the new republic, use of the words "slave" and "slavery" was carefully avoided in the original document. Political representation in the lower House of Congress was to be based on the population of "free Persons" in each state, plus three-fifths of all "other Persons." Moral principles against slavery, for those who had them, were compromised, with no explanation of the conflicting principles for which the American Revolutionary War had ostensibly been fought: the self-evident truths "that all men are created equal, that they are endowed by their Creator with certain unalienable Rights, that among these are Life, Liberty, and the Pursuit of Happiness."

It was not the first such compromise. Even these ringing phrases from the Declaration of Independence are filled with irony, for an early draft of what became that declaration assailed the King of England for suppressing legislative attempts to end the slave trade and for encouraging slave rebellions. The final draft adopted in 1776 did not contain this criticism. And so again at the Constitutional Convention eloquent objections to the institution of slavery went unheeded, and its opponents eventually consented to a document which laid a foundation for the tragic events that were to follow.

Pennsylvania's Gouverneur Morris provides an example. He opposed slavery and the counting of slaves in determining the basis for representation in Congress. At the Convention he objected that

> The inhabitant of Georgia [or] South Carolina who goes to the coast of Africa, and in defiance of the most sacred laws of humanity tears away his fellow creatures from their dearest connections and damns them to the most cruel bondages, shall have more votes in a government instituted for protection of the rights of mankind, than the Citizen of Pennsylvania or New Jersey who views with a laudable horror, so nefarious a practice.

And yet Gouverneur Morris eventually accepted the three-fifths accommodation. In fact, he wrote the final draft of the Constitution, the very document the bicentennial will commemorate.

As a result of the compromise, the right of the Southern states to continue importing slaves was extended, officially, at least until 1808. We know that it actually lasted a good deal longer, as the framers possessed no monopoly on the ability to trade moral principles for self-interest. But they nevertheless set an unfortunate example. Slaves could be imported, if the commercial interests of the North were protected. To make the compromise even more palatable, customs duties would be imposed at up to ten dollars per slave as a means of raising public revenues.

No doubt it will be said, when the unpleasant truth of the history of slavery in America is mentioned during this bicentennial year, that the Constitution was a product of its times, and embodied a compromise which, under other circumstances, would not have been made. But the effects of the framers' compromise have remained for generations. They arose from the contradiction between guaranteeing liberty and justice to all, and denying both to Negroes.

The original intent of the phrase "We the People," was far too clear for any ameliorating construction. Writing for the Supreme Court in 1857, Chief Justice Taney penned the following passage in the *Dred Scott* case, on the issue of whether, in the eyes of the framers, slaves were "constituent members of the sovereignty," and were to be included among "We the People":

> We think they are not, and that they are not included, and were not intended to be included***

They had for more than a century before been regarded as beings of an inferior order, and altogether unfit to associate with the white race ***; and so far inferior, that they had no rights which the white man was bound to respect; and that the negro might justly and lawfully be reduced to slavery for his benefit ***

[A]ccordingly, a negro of the African race was regarded *** as an article of property, and held, and bought and sold as such *** [N]o one seems to have doubted the correctness of the prevailing opinion of the time.

And so, nearly seven decades after the Constitutional Convention, the Supreme Court reaffirmed the prevailing opinion of the framers regarding the rights of Negroes in America. It took a bloody civil war before the thirteenth amendment could be adopted to abolish slavery, though not the consequences slavery would have for future Americans.

While the Union survived the civil war, the Constitution did not. In its place arose a new, more promising basis for justice and equality, the fourteenth amendment, ensuring protection of the life, liberty, and property of *all* persons against deprivations without due process, and guaranteeing equal protection of the laws. And yet almost another century would pass before any significant recognition was obtained of the rights of black Americans to share equally even in such basic opportunities as education, housing, and employment, and to have their votes counted, and counted equally. In the meantime, blacks joined America's military to fight its wars and invested untold hours working in its factories and on its farms, contributing to the development of this country's magnificent wealth and waiting to share in its prosperity.

What is striking is the role legal principles have played throughout America's history in determining the condition of Negroes. They were enslaved by law, emancipated by law, disenfranchised and segregated by law; and finally, they have begun to win equality by law. Along the way, new constitutional principles have emerged to meet the challenges of a changing society. The progress has been dramatic, and it will continue.

The men who gathered in Philadelphia in 1787 could not have envisioned these changes. They could not have imagined, nor would they have accepted, that the document they were drafting would one day be constructed by a Supreme Court to which had been appointed a woman and the descendent of an African slave. "We the People" no longer enslave, but the credit does not belong to the framers. It belongs to those who refused to acquiesce in outdated notions of "liberty," "justice," and "equality," and who strived to better them.

And so we must be careful, when focusing on the events which took place in Philadelphia two centuries ago, that we not overlook the momentous events which followed, and thereby lose our proper sense of perspective. Otherwise, the odds are that for many Americans the bicentennial celebration will be little more than a blind pilgrimage to the shrine of the original document now stored in a vault in the National Archives. If we seek, instead, a sensitive understanding of the Constitution's inherent defects and its promising evolution through 200 years of history, the celebration of the "Miracle at Philadelphia" will, in my view, be a far more meaningful and humbling experience. We will see that the true miracle was not the birth of the Constitution, but its life, a life nurtured through two turbulent centuries of our own making, and a life embodying much good fortune that was not.

Thus, in this bicentennial year, we may not all participate in the festivities with flag-waving fervor. Some may more quietly commemorate the suffering, struggle, and sacrifice that has triumphed over much of what was wrong with the original document, and observe the anniversary with hopes not realized and promises not fulfilled. I plan to celebrate the bicentennial of the Constitution as a living document, including the Bill of Rights and the other amendments protecting individual freedoms and human rights.

QUESTIONS

1. Reflect upon your own view of the Constitution. Do you consider it a miraculous achievement for its time, or do you see it as merely a solid product that luckily changed much for the better over the course of American history?

2. Is Marshall too tough – or not tough enough – on the Framers? Does he give them sufficient credit for their handiwork? Is he sensitive enough to the political realities and standards of the times in which they crafted the Constitution?

3. The Framers certainly were Enlightenment thinkers with high ideals, but they also were practical politicians. Do you believe that it was necessary for them to accept the institution of slavery so that the new Constitution could come into being? If so, did they do the right thing? Or, should they have rejected this compromise and stood their ground – even if this would have meant the rejection of the Constitution?

CHAPTER 6

TRUMAN VS. MACARTHUR

Walter Karp

Walter Karp recounts the events leading up to and following President Truman's decision to fire General Douglas MacArthur. General MacArthur's enormous popularity made this decision a particularly risky political move. More importantly by firing MacArthur, Truman assserted and affirmed military subordination to civilian political authority. This famous clash dramatizes this historic problem of civil-military relations and underscores the ethical reasons underlying the Constitutional provisions to keep the military out of the politics of governing.

At 1:00 A.M. on the morning of April 11, 1951, a tense band of Washington reporters filed into the White House newsroom for an emergency press conference. Hastily summoned by the White House switchboard, they had no idea of what was to come. The Truman administration, detested by millions, had grown hesitant, timid, and unpredictable. The Korean War, so boldly begun ten months before, had degenerated into a "limited war" with no discernible limit, a bloody stalemate. Some reporters, guessing, thought they were going to hear about a declaration of war, that the administration was ready to carry the fighting into China and bring it to a swift and victorious end. That was what Gen. Douglas MacArthur, supreme commander of U.S. and United Nations forces in the Far East, had passionately been urging for months, ever since Chinese communist troops had sent his armies reeling in retreat from the Yalu River.

President Truman did not appear in the newsroom. His press secretary merely handed out copies of three terse presidential statements. At 1:03 A.M. the great wire-service networks were carrying the news to the ends of the earth. The President had not adopted the victory plans of America's greatest living general. Instead he had relieved him of all his commands, "effective at once." The President had acted because "General of the Army Douglas MacArthur is unable to give his wholehearted support to the policies of the United States and the United Nations."

With that announcement President Truman precipitated perhaps the most convulsive popular outburst in American history and the severest test which civilian control of the military has ever had to face in this republic. On April 11 there was little reason to believe that the faltering President would triumph over his vaunting general in the clash that must ensue.

Even before the news broke, the American people were upset. "A vast impatience, a turbulent bitterness, a rancor akin to revolt" coursed through the body politic, a contemporary historian observed. Dislike of communism, once a matter of course in America, had boiled into a national frenzy, devouring common prudence, common sense, and common decency. It was a time when school textbooks urged children to report suspicious neighbors to the FBI "in line with American tradition," a time when an entire city flew into a rage on learning that the geography lesson printed on children's candy wrappers dared to describe Russia as the "largest country in the world." Americans saw conspiracy in every untoward event: abroad, "Kremlin plots to conquer the world"; at home, communist plots to "take over the government." In April 1951 a substantial part of the citizenry believed that the secretary of state, Dean Acheson, was a "dupe" of the Kremlin, that the secretary of defense, George C. Marshall, a five-star general, was a "front man" for traitors in government. And now it seemed that a great general, World War II's most glamorous hero, had been mercilessly broken for daring to call for victory in Korea.

On the morning of April 11 only Western Union's rules of propriety kept Congress from being deluged with furious obscenity. "Impeach the B who calls himself President," read one telegram typical of those pouring into Washington at an unprecedented rate—125,000 within forty-eight hours. "Impeach the little ward politician stupidity from Kansas City," read another, voicing the contempt millions now felt for the "plucky Harry" of just a few years before. The letters and telegrams, the White House admitted, were running 20 to 1 against the President. So were the telephone calls that jangled in every newsroom and radio studio. In countless towns the President was hanged in effigy. Across the country flags flew at half-mast or upside down. Angry signs blossomed on houses: "To hell with the Reds and Harry Truman."

Wherever politicians met that day, the anger in the streets was echoed and amplified. In Los Angeles the city council adjourned for the day "in sorrowful contemplation of the political assassination of General MacArthur." In Michigan the state legislature solemnly noted that "at 1:00 A.M. of this day, World Communism achieved its greatest victory of a decade in the dismissal of General MacArthur." On the Senate floor in Washington, Republicans took turns denouncing the President: "I charge that this country today is in the hands of a secret inner coterie which is directed by agents of the Soviet Union. We must cut this whole cancerous conspiracy out of our Government at once," said William Jenner of Indiana. Truman had given "the Communists and their stooges . . . what they always wanted—MacArthur's scalp." So spoke the country's fastest-rising politician, Richard Nixon. Only four senators—two Democrats and two Republicans—dared defend the President.

For most Republican leaders in Congress the popular hysteria was manna in the political desert. Their best men—Ohio's Robert Taft most conspicuously— had felt doomed to perpetual impotence, spurned by an electorate that still revered the memory, and supported the policies, of the late Franklin Roosevelt. Now they saw their chance. They were determined to discredit the Democratic party and its stumbling President. At a hasty meeting on the morning of MacArthur's dismissal, Republican congressional leaders came to a decision. They intended to use every political resource at their disposal to channel popular anger over MacArthur's recall into a mass revolt against "limited war," against President Truman and the ghost of the Roosevelt New Deal.

It was a reckless decision: exalting MacArthur over the President, as Harold Ickes, the old Bull Moose Republican, was to warn a few days later, would set a "precedent" that would "develop into a monstrosity"—an uncontrollable military.

Such, in truth, were the stakes now at hazard. In the four months preceding his dismissal, General MacArthur had transgressed the fundamental rule of civilian supremacy, a rule given its classic formulation in Lincoln's stern instructions to Grant: "You are not to decide, discuss or confer with anyone or ask political questions; such questions the President holds in his own hands, and will submit them to no military conferences or conventions." What MacArthur had done was to carry out a public political campaign designed to discredit the President's policies and compel the White House to follow his own. For that the President had ordered his recall. If that recall were to end by destroying the President, if MacArthur, backed by a wave of popular support, were to force his policies on the civil authority, then for all practical purposes civilian supremacy over the military would become a dead letter. Given such a precedent, what future President would dare dismiss a popular general in wartime for publicly challenging his authority?

When the Republican meeting broke up at 10:00 A.M., the press was informed of the plan to exalt the general over the President. Republicans intended to demand a full-dress investigation of the President's war policies. That was remarkable enough considering that it was wartime. The second element in their plan, however, was more than remarkable. It had no precedent in our history. Republicans intended (if Democratic votes were forthcoming) to invite General MacArthur to address a joint session of Congress, the most august assembly the United States can provide. In the well of the House of Representatives, where only a handful of foreign statesmen and homecoming heroes had ever been allowed to speak, a rebellious, contumacious general was to be given his chance to defend his cause against the President of the United States.

What would MacArthur do? In Germany, General Eisenhower, supreme commander of Allied forces in Europe, expressed the sentiments of a good many Americans. He hoped the seventy-one-year-old general, his onetime superior, would drift quietly into retirement. "I would not like to see acrimony," Eisenhower remarked somewhat wistfully to a reporter. In fact, there was no chance that MacArthur would not carry his fight to the country.

By any standard General MacArthur was an awesome and prodigious figure. He possessed an uncommonly powerful intellect, one sharpened by vast erudition, intense meditation, and an extraordinary facility with words. He was utterly fearless, unshakably self-possessed, and relentlessly willful. At the White House the President had shrunk from confronting him for months. Moreover, MacArthur's strengths were magnified by the aura surrounding him. He was dramatic, compelling, aloof, and imperious, qualities he himself had cultivated with all the theatrical arts at his command. What was to govern his conduct in the ensuing months, however, were not his great gifts but a bitter flaw in his character—a blind, all-consuming vanity.

The general was vain in small ways; the famous MacArthur sunglasses, for example, disguised the prosaic fact of myopia. He was vain in his choice of associates; his entourage consisted of toadies and idolators. Vanity even colored his conceptions of grand strategy; the center of the world for MacArthur was always the military theater under his command. During World War II his military colleagues used to say the general had a bad case of "localitis." Vanity sometimes drove him to the borders of paranoia: a lifetime of triumphs could not efface his belief that homefront "cabals" were plotting his ruin, that "insidious forces" were stabbing him in the back. His worst enemies, MacArthur often said, had "always been behind me." Vanity led him, too, to that most perilous of convictions—an absolute faith in his own infallibility. Therein lay the crux of the matter, for that faith had been brutally assaulted five months earlier when MacArthur's armies, poised for victory near the Yalu River, had fallen into a colossal Chinese trap. On November 24, 1950, America's greatest military strategist had presided over one of the worst defeats in the history of American arms. From that day forward General MacArthur was a man thirsting for vindication and vengeance. To drive the Chinese out of North Korea had become a fixed and obsessive goal. To break the administration that stood in his way had now become, of necessity, his political object. "He did not want facts or logic," as a longtime admirer, Carlos Romulo of the Philippines, was to put it after an interview with the general. "He wanted salve for his wounded pride." That was a dangerous motive, indeed, for a general who had become, overnight, the second most powerful man in America.

In the last years of the Roman Republic, people had watched with mounting tension as Pompey the Great made his triumphal return home from the East. So it was in America in mid-April of 1951 as MacArthur prepared to depart from Tokyo on his personal plane, the *Bataan.*

On April 13 Americans learned that the general, hastening his return, intended to reach America within a few days, destroying the hopes of the President's supporters that the popular fury would abate before MacArthur set foot on native soil. That day, too, Democratic leaders, under popular pressure, gave up their struggle to prevent Congress from inviting MacArthur to address a joint session. One slightly comical concession was all they would wrest from the onrushing Republican minority: officially the general would be addressing not a "joint session" but a "joint meeting."

On Sunday, April 15, newspaper headlines told of MacArthur's "triumphant goodby" from Japan, of the crowds lining the streets, of the Japanese dignitaries on hand for the departure. The triumphal progress had now begun, its ultimate destination the nation's capital, where, at exactly 12:30 P.M. on the nineteenth, it was now announced, the general would enter the House of Representatives and throw down his gauntlet to the President. Bulletins flashing over the nation's radios marked the progress of the general's plane. At 1:00 A.M. Eastern time on Monday, the *Bataan* passed over Wake Island; first stop, Honolulu. If the general was in official disgrace, there was no sign of it: at the Hawaiian capital MacArthur and his wife and thirteen-year-old son stopped over for twenty-four hours as the guest of Adm. Arthur W. Radford, commander in chief of America's naval forces in the Pacific. At Honolulu University the general received an honorary degree in civil law, an ironic honor considering that its recipient had by now convinced himself—as he was soon to say—that American generals had the constitutional right to say whatever they pleased in public regardless of the orders of their commander in chief. Far away in New York, the city fathers announced plans to greet the general with the biggest parade in the history of that city of ticker-tape acclamations.

On the evening of April 17 General MacArthur's plane touched down at San Francisco's airport, ending the general's fourteen-year absence from his country. At the airport ten thousand people, desperate for a glimpse of their hero, surged past police barricades, mobbing the general and his entourage. It was "an indescribable scene of pandemonium," one of MacArthur's aides recalled. Tens of thousands of automobiles jammed the roads for miles around, creating the worst traffic snarl in San Francisco's history. A half-million people lined the route from the airport to MacArthur's hotel, where a powerful police cordon alone kept the general from being trampled by his admirers. Twenty-eight hours later, at Washington's National Airport, pandemonium broke loose again with surging mobs, tumultuous cheers, and a battered police cordon trying to clear a space around the general, who remained, as always, calm and unruffled, the eye of the hurricane he had created.

At the White House the President took cold comfort from his professed belief that Americans were *not* hailing an insubordinate general nor embracing his "victory" policy but merely giving a belated welcome to the last World War II hero to return to America. Like the "joint meeting" of Congress, now just hours away, it was a distinction apparent to few.

At 12:31 P.M. on April 19 a record thirty million people tuned in their radios to hear General MacArthur address Congress, his countrymen, and the world. This was the moment every supporter of the President had dreaded. Truman's case for a limited war of attrition had not yet been effectively made. Half the country was not even aware that attrition was the chosen policy of the government. Even well-informed supporters of the President were not sure what the policy meant or why it was necessary. Now General MacArthur, backed by an adoring nation and armed with high gifts of intellect and eloquence, was about to speak against it.

"I address you with neither rancor nor bitterness in the fading twilight of life," the general began in his vibrant, well-modulated voice after the wild initial ovation had subsided. MacArthur devoted the first half of his speech to a lofty and lucid disquisition on the politics and destiny of Asia. His object, he said, was to dispel the prevailing "unreality" of American thinking on the subject. His authority established, MacArthur proceeded to praise the administration for intervening in Korea—the only time that Democrats in the audience had a chance to applaud—and for attempting to drive the communists out of North Korea. That objective had lain in his grasp when the Chinese communists intervened in the struggle. "This created a new war and an entirely new situation." Yet the administration was not fighting that new war to win. It was not attempting to "defeat this new enemy as we had defeated the old." By confining the war against Chinese aggression to Korea, it was condemning the country to "prolonged indecision."

Yet the means to achieve victory were swift and sure. Three quite moderate military measures would drive the Chinese from the Korean peninsula: bombing China's "sanctuaries" in Manchuria; blockading the Chinese coast; unleashing Chiang Kai-shek's army, holed up in Formosa, for diversionary raids on the Chinese mainland. Such was MacArthur's plan "to bring hostilities to a close with the least possible delay." What was there to be said against it? "In war, indeed, there is no substitute for victory," said MacArthur, providing his supporters with their most potent slogan. "'Why,' my soldiers asked of me, 'surrender military advantages to an enemy in the field?'" MacArthur's voice fell to a whisper: "I could not answer." Why fight Red China without attempting to drive her from Korea? This was a policy of "appeasement," said the general, hurling the deadliest epithet of the day at the Truman administration. Moreover, said MacArthur, his plan to carry the war to the Chinese mainland had been supported by "our own Joint Chiefs of Staff." With that assertion Republicans in the House gave the speaker a thunderous standing ovation, for, in fact, it was the most devastating remark in MacArthur's entire speech. In the prevailing atmosphere of derangement and conspiracy it implied that victory in Korea had been snatched from America's grasp not by the military judgment of the Pentagon but by a mere, meddlesome civilian, the President of the United States. MacArthur's assertion also posed a challenge to the Joint Chiefs themselves: he was daring them to side with the President when, as he fully believed, their purely military judgment agreed with his own.

For close observers that was the real news of the hour, the story that made the headlines. What stirred the rest of the country, however, was MacArthur's lush, emotional peroration. He recalled the old barracks ballad that "proclaimed, most proudly, that 'Old soldiers never die. They just fade away.' And like the soldier of the ballad, I now close my military career and just fade away—an old soldier who tried to do his duty as God gave him the light to see that duty." And then in a hushed voice: "Good-bye."

Generals in the audience openly wept. Legislators hurled themselves at the departing general, virtually prostrating themselves at his feet. "It's disloyal not to agree with General MacArthur!" one senator shouted from the floor. "We have heard God speak today. God in the flesh, the voice of God," shouted Rep. Dewey Short of Missouri, who had been educated at Harvard, Oxford, and Heidelberg. The normally levelheaded former President Herbert Hoover hailed MacArthur as the "reincarnation of St. Paul." Fury over his dismissal boiled up anew and newspaper offices again were besieged with vehement calls condemning the "traitorous" State Department and the "bankrupt haberdasher" who was "appeasing Red China." It boiled up, too, on the floor of the House. As one senator confided to a reporter later that day: "I have never feared more for the institutions of the country. I honestly felt that if the speech had gone on much longer there might have been a march on the White House."

MacArthur's powerful speech, a magniloquent contrast to the President's pawky little lectures, "visibly and profoundly shook" the President's supporters in Congress, as the *New York Times* reported. The President's cabinet, after watching MacArthur on a White House television set, sank into gloom, convinced that the general, in a single blow, had put a finish to the Truman administration. The welcoming parade for the general in New York City confirmed their worst fears.

MacArthur flew to the city on the evening of the nineteenth, settling into what was to be his home for the remaining thirteen years of his life: a palatial ten-room suite on the thirty-seventh floor of the Waldorf-Astoria. The hotel was to be the parade's point of departure. The general would be driven in an open car—the same that had carried General Eisenhower six years before—through Central Park, down to the Battery, up through the canyons of Wall Street, and homeward along Fifth Avenue—over nineteen miles in all. The triumphal progress was to begin at 11:00 A.M., but by dawn hundreds of thousands of people had already begun pouring into the city. By the time the general's motorcade had reached the financial district, some six million flag-waving enthusiasts were jamming the sidewalks, dwarfing Eisenhower's postwar parade and Lindbergh's almost legendary reception. Overhead in the bright, cloudless sky, airplanes spelled out "Welcome Home" in mile-long streamers. Shreds of paper fell in dense blizzards, covering people's feet to the ankles and darkening television screens for minutes at a time. As the general's car approached, the crowds craned hungrily forward, then burst into cheers, deafening in their volume, startling in their intensity. Not everyone shouted his acclaim. There were people who watched the general pass by in silence, faces rapt and grim, marking a cross on their breasts. New York, as MacArthur's bodyguard was to put it, had been turned into "a band of hysterical sheep"— hard- bitten, cynical New York, stronghold of the Democratic party.

Late that afternoon, while the general was passing up howling Fifth Avenue, a popular demonstration of a different sort took place at a baseball park in the nation's capital. As the President and his entourage were about to leave Griffith Stadium—Truman had thrown out the traditional first ball of the year—he was met with a storm of boos. Republicans were now saying the choice before the country was "Truman or MacArthur"; on April 20, Americans seemed already to have made it.

In his struggle with MacArthur, the President faced severe handicaps, most of them self-inflicted. The political derangement of the country was to a large extent his own doing. Determined to arouse the nation to the menace of Soviet expansion, yet convinced that he governed an obstinately "isolationist" people, Truman had never scrupled to exaggerate every danger, to sound alarms, to decry in any communist move he opposed another step in the "Kremlin plot for world conquest." Moreover, he had constantly used the great World War II generals—MacArthur included—to defend his policies and shield him from criticism. The results were inevitable. Because Truman had glorified the wisdom of the generals, he had weakened the civilian authority he was now forced to defend. Because he justified even prudent deeds with inflammatory words, it had become difficult to justify prudent deeds with prudent arguments—the sort of argument he was now forced to make.

The President's inept handling of the Korean War was the severest handicap of all. In June 1950 Truman had intervened to repel the North Korean invasion of South Korea, an essentially defensive objective. When North Korean armies began fleeing back beyond the thirty-eighth parallel, however, Truman made a momentous and disastrous decision. He directed General MacArthur to cross the parallel and liberate North Korea from communist control too. Thus it was Truman, not MacArthur, who had first defined victory in Korea as the extirpation of communism from the entire Korean peninsula. When four hundred thousand Chinese entered the fray, however, the administration changed its mind again. Without informing the electorate, Truman decided that liberating North Korea— victory—was a prize not worth the terrible risks involved. He was now content to confine the fighting to Korea until exhausted Chinese armies eventually decided to call it a day at the thirty-eighth parallel. The administration, in short, was fighting to restore Korea to the situation it had been in on the eve of the North Korean invasion—at the cost of sixty thousand American casualties by mid-April and with no truce in sight.

Such was the policy the administration now had to defend in the court of inflamed public opinion against the clarity and emotional force of MacArthur's crisp plan for "victory." In two major radio addresses, the President's first attempts to make a case for his policy proved ineffective. His two chief arguments simply lacked conviction. First, the bombing of Chinese supply lines would, he said, lead to a general war in Asia and possibly to World War III. Here a large majority of Americans simply preferred MacArthur's military judgment to the President's. Moreover, in citing the risks involved, Truman was compelled to argue that Korea was not all that important compared with the defense of Europe. The President, in effect, was belittling his own war, which did nothing to strengthen popular confidence in his judgment.

Truman's second argument was even less convincing. The stalemated war, he insisted, was already a resounding success. It had stopped in its tracks, said the President, the Kremlin's "carefully prepared plot for conquering all of Asia." It had "slowed down the timetable of conquest," he assured the country, invoking memories of Hitler's step-by-step conquest of Europe. Since the Kremlin "timetable" was entirely suppositious, the President could offer no evidence whatever of its alleged slowdown.

Republicans had no trouble tearing the President's speeches to shreds. They simply turned Truman's own Cold War propaganda against him. Time and again the administration had argued that "punishing aggression" in Korea was preventing World War III—more echoes of the Hitler years. If so, Republicans now argued, then why was the President unwilling to punish the Chinese aggressors. It was the President's "half-war" against Red China, not MacArthur's plan for victory, that was inviting World War III. As for the President's apparent willingness to settle for a truce at the thirty-eighth parallel, it would be a "sellout," a "super-Munich."

Most of all, Republicans struck at the very notion of fighting a "limited war." It was, wrote *Time,* "an idea unique in world history, that it is wrong and dangerous to fight the enemy in any place not of the enemy's choosing." It meant sacrificing American lives on "an altar of futility." It meant giving the enemy "privileged sanctuaries" outside Korea from which to kill American boys more effectively. It "shocks our national sense of decency," said Sen. Henry Cabot Lodge, himself no friend of MacArthur's. "Psychologically, no one will stand for it," said Senator Taft, sadly abandoning his lifelong opposition to excessive overseas commitments.

Keenly aware of his fading powers of persuasion, Truman countered with dubious blows of his own. He "leaked" to the *New York Times* the secret White House notes of his October 15, 1950, meeting with MacArthur at Wake Island, a meeting in which, said the notes, MacArthur had confidently assured the President that there was "very little" chance of Chinese intervention in Korea. Stung for the first time, MacArthur retorted from the Waldorf that the administration, too, had misread Chinese intentions, although it had far greater intelligence resources than a mere theater commander possessed. This was quite true. Blaming MacArthur for disastrously misleading the President was grossly unfair, but "politics isn't beanbag," as Mr. Dooley had long before observed. A few days after the "leak," MacArthur once again demonstrated his extraordinary hold on his countrymen. A flying trip to the Midwest on April 26 brought in the latest returns from the grass roots: three million acclaimed him in Chicago, one million in Milwaukee. The general had not "faded away," but five different versions of "Old Soldiers Never Die" were now blaring from America's jukeboxes.

The stage was now set for the second half of the Republican campaign to exalt the general over the President. This was the forthcoming congressional investigation of the administration's Far Eastern policies, with the general as star witness for the Republican prosecution. Nobody knew at the time that the hearings would mark the beginning of the end for MacArthur. The confident Republicans demanded public, televised hearings, the largest possible audience for their hero and their weapon. Equally convinced of the President's weakness and none too sure of the Joint Chiefs of Staff, the Democrats fought desperately to keep the hearings secret, piously citing the need to prevent high matters of state from reaching enemy ears. It took several days of bitter parliamentary strife before the ground rules of the hearings were finally laid down. They were to be conducted jointly by the Senate Armed Services and Foreign Relations Committees—fourteen Democrats and twelve Republicans in all. Press, public, and even the House of Representatives were to be strictly excluded, but censored transcripts of the testimony would be released every hour to an avid public. In the very midst of war the military policies of the United States were to be subjected to intense and critical scrutiny as the struggle between President and general moved into the arena of a Senate caucus room. It was, as the *New York Times* put it, a "debate unprecedented in American and probably world history."

On the morning of May 3 the huge wooden doors of the caucus room banged shut on a horde of newsmen as General of the Army Douglas MacArthur took his seat as the hearing's first witness. Every major newspaper in the country planned to print his entire testimony. In the witness chair, *Time* noted, the general's "self- confidence was monumental." He carried no notes, consulted no aides, and answered every question without the slightest hesitation. While Democratic senators fumbled with their queries, he calmly puffed on a briar pipe.

As expected, he hit the administration hard. What was unexpected were his passionate outbursts. In a voice charged with emotion he accused the government again and again of wantonly squandering American lives. "I shrink—shrink with a horror that I cannot express in words—at this continuous slaughter of men. . . . Are you going to let that go by any sophistry of reasoning?" Administration arguments he dealt with skillfully. Its contention that a win-the-war policy would cost us our European allies he termed a mere pretext; the United States was already doing most of the fighting in Korea. Its contention that Russia, not China, was America's main enemy he adroitly denied by using the Truman Doctrine against Truman: the enemy was not Russia but "communism all over the world." He belittled the danger of Soviet intervention on Red China's behalf. It was the administration's policy of "appeasement" that invited aggression.

Once again MacArthur insisted that the Joint Chiefs had agreed with his plan. Their views and his were "practically identical." He even cited an official document that seemed to prove it: a January 12 memorandum from the Chiefs "tentatively" agreeing to some of the measures against China that the general was advocating. To MacArthur the document was conclusive. On January 12, 1951, the Joint Chiefs of Staff had not been persuaded by the "sophistry of reasoning" now being woven by the "politicians," MacArthur's contemptuous— and revealing—term for the civil government of the United States.

As propaganda in a war of headlines, MacArthur's three days of testimony proved powerful indeed. Nonetheless it revealed much that would soon prove detrimental to the general and his cause. Americans acclaimed him as a great military strategist, yet as a witness he sounded like a man so obsessed with striking back at China that he seemed deliberately blind to the risks. Americans saw him as an honest soldier, yet he often sounded like a demagogue. In the Senate caucus room it was already becoming clear, like a photograph slowly developing, that MacArthur was no martyred hero but an extraordinarily ambitious and self-willed general. Whether the bulk of the electorate would come to see this was anybody's guess.

Everything depended on the next series of Senate witnesses, namely the President's principal military advisers: Gen. George C. Marshall, secretary of defense; Gen. Omar Bradley, chairman of the Joint Chiefs of Staff; and the three service chiefs composing that body. This was the supreme irony of the political crisis. In the spring of 1951 the fate of civilian control of the military was absolutely dependent on the military's unswerving fidelity to that principle. It was not merely a matter of swearing fealty to the rule at the hearings. It was not even enough to endorse in a general way the President's policy of limited war. MacArthur's challenge to the President was too powerful for half-measures. The military chiefs would have to do what MacArthur was certain they would never do, what he believed them too "professional" to do. They would have to appear in the caucus room, before hostile senators, and concede absolutely nothing to General MacArthur. If they harbored doubts about limited war, they would have to keep such sentiments to themselves. If they saw merit in any of MacArthur's arguments, they would have to refuse, nonetheless, to acknowledge it. To the intense relief of the President's supporters, that is exactly what they proceeded to do.

Truman's five military spokesmen spent nineteen days in the witness chair, nineteen days in which MacArthur's conduct, MacArthur's victory plan, and even MacArthur's military reputation were ceaselessly battered. Was MacArthur's dismissal warranted? It was more than warranted; it was absolutely necessary. "General MacArthur's actions were continuing to jeopardize civilian control over military affairs." His public campaign to discredit the President's policies "was against all custom and tradition for a military man." What was wrong with MacArthur's victory plan? It would not bring victory "but a larger deadlock at greater expense." Would bombing Chinese "sanctuaries" help decisively in Korea? No, but it would leave America's home air defenses "naked." What of the Joint Chiefs' now-celebrated January 12 memorandum? The military chiefs brushed it aside. It was contingent on imminent defeat in Korea, and that contingency had long since passed. Never for a single moment had the Joint Chiefs of Staff subscribed to MacArthur's plan for victory. What about "the deification of this infallible leader," asked Sen. William Fulbright. Had he not blundered at the Yalu when he walked into a Chinese trap? Apparently he had—a stunning accusation. As James Reston of the *New York Times* observed: "MacArthur started as the prosecutor and is now the defendant."

It was General Bradley, a genuine World War II hero and a man untainted by political controversy, who delivered the heaviest blows and the only quotable remark the administration managed to coin. MacArthur's plan, said Bradley, would involve the United States in "the wrong war at the wrong time with the wrong enemy." That was on May 15, Bradley's first day of testimony, with more of the same to come. Republican senators were stunned. Blindly trusting MacArthur, they simply had not expected the Pentagon to line up behind Truman's policies with such uncompromising zeal. Still less had they expected the Joint Chiefs to belittle their great colleague's military reputation or to accuse him, as General Marshall did, of undermining the morale of American combat troops by his condemnation of the war they were fighting. Republican leaders had underestimated not only the military's fidelity to "custom and tradition" but also the intense personal dislike that the imperious MacArthur had inspired in his World War II colleagues.

The testimony of the military chiefs was by no means unimpeachable. It was often glib and evasive. It was certainly no model of candor. Yet it was quite obvious to contemporaries that Republican committee members did little to discredit their testimony. Exalting MacArthur had been reckless enough. Blackening the Joint Chiefs of Staff in wartime was more than most Republicans had the heart to attempt. Already there were mutterings from the party professionals—national committeemen meeting in Tulsa—that the MacArthur affair might "boomerang" and leave Republicans looking like the "war party" for the 1952 elections. When General Bradley completed his testimony, Republicans lamely proposed that no more generals be called. The

CHAPTER 7

"THE RETURN OF PRAGMATISM"

Louis Menand.

Alexis De Tocqueville observed that Americans are quite concerned with the here-and-now, with achieving things in the real world. Theory for its own sake has never been Americans' strong suit; indeed, as Louis Menand observes, "Philosophies and theories and formal methodologies are part of our culture, but they are the dinner jacket and bow tie we instinctively take off when it is time to change the tires." It should come as no surprise, then, that pragmatism is the unique American contribution to the field of philosophy. Over the past century, the culture, legal system, and education system of the United States all have been shaped powerfully by this school of thought. Menand explains the genesis and evolution of American pragmatism, including a marked renewal of interest in it in recent years.

In ordinary speech, pragmatism connotes practicality, common sense, feet on the ground -- virtues Americans like to think of as specifically American virtues. One thing the term does not connote is philosophical speculation. When we say someone is pragmatic, we are usually implying that he or she is not given to abstract rumination. But pragmatism is also the name of a particular type of philosophy. It was first introduced publicly nearly a hundred years ago, in 1898, by William James, and for several decades arguments over it dominated American philosophy. Then, in the 1930s, it went into a long period of eclipse, almost forgotten amid the emergence of new philosophical schools and theoretical paradigms. But since 1980 it has made an astonishing comeback. Legal writers, literary critics, historians, political theorists, and educators -- not to mention philosophers -- are starting to call themselves pragmatists. And by that term they mean to invoke the philosophical tradition of a century ago. Why is it back? What was it? Where did it come from? Pragmatism is an account of the way people think. This may not seem like a terribly useful thing to have. After all, if pragmatism's account of the way people think is accurate, then we are already thinking the way pragmatists tell us we are. Why would we need a description of something we do anyway without it? It is as though someone were to offer us an account of the way our hair grows with the promise that having it will give us nicer hair. But pragmatists don't believe there is a problem with the way people think. They believe there is a problem with the way people think they think. They believe, in other words, that other accounts of the way people think are mistaken;

they believe that these mistaken accounts are responsible for a large number of conceptual puzzles; and they believe that these puzzles, when they are not simply wasting the energy of the people who spend their time trying to solve them, actually get in the way of our everyday efforts to cope with the world. Pragmatism is therefore an effort to unhitch human beings from what pragmatists regard as a useless structure of bad abstractions about thought. The sheer bravado of the attempt, the suggestion that all we need to do to lighten our load is just drop the whole contraption over the side of a cliff and continue on doing what we want to be doing anyway, makes pragmatist writing exhilarating to read. The classic pragmatist essays -- Charles Sanders Peirce's "How to Make Our Ideas Clear," William James's "The Will to Believe," Oliver Wendell Holmes's "The Path of the Law," Richard Rorty's "Philosophy as a Kind of Writing" -- have a kind of ground-clearing sweep to them that gives many readers the sense that a pressing but vaguely understood obligation has suddenly been lifted from their shoulders, that some final examination for which they could never possibly have felt prepared has just been canceled.

What has seemed liberating to some readers has, of course, seemed to others like negligence and worse. The nonchalance with which pragmatists tend to dispose of issues that have engaged other thinkers has always struck many people as intellectually slipshod and morally dangerous. "Pragmatism is a matter of human needs," wrote G. K. Chesterton in 1908, when international interest in pragmatism was first at its height, "and one of the first of human needs is to be something more than a pragmatist." If the pragmatist account is correct, warned Bertrand Russell a year later, then "ironclads and Maxim guns must be the ultimate arbiters of metaphysical truth." Pragmatists today have attracted similar sorts of hostility....

Pragmatists -- and this, to their critics, may be the most irritating thing about them -- love these objections.... They confirm what the pragmatist has always claimed, which is that what people believe to be true is just what they think it is good to believe to be true. The critic who argues from the consequences of accepting the pragmatist account of the way we think -- the critic who warns that dumping those other accounts over a cliff will lead to despair, war, illiberalism, or political correctness -- has (in the pragmatist's view) already conceded the key point, which is that every account of the way people think is, at bottom, a support for those human goods the person making the account believes to be important. The whole force of a philosophical account of anything, pragmatists insist, lies in the advertised consequences of accepting it. When we say to a child, "That's the way the world is," we are not making a neutral report. We are saying that understanding the world in that way will put the child into a better relation with it, will enable him or her to cope with it more satisfactorily -- even if it means recognizing how unsatisfactory, from a child's point of view (or anyone's), the world can be.

What is pragmatism's account of the way people think, and how did it arise?

The term was introduced to the world by William James in a lecture called "Philosophical Conceptions and Practical Results," which he delivered on a visit to the University of California at Berkeley in 1898. James presented what he called "the principle of Peirce, the principle of pragmatism," which he defined as follows: "To attain perfect clearness in our thoughts of an object . . . we need only consider what effects of a conceivably practical kind the object may involve -- what sensations we are to expect from it, and what reactions we must prepare. Our conception of these effects, then, is for us the whole of our conception of the object, so far as that conception has positive significance at all." He went on to suggest that this principle might be expressed "more broadly," and he proceeded to do so: "The ultimate test for us of what a truth means is indeed the conduct it dictates or inspires.... the effective meaning of any philosophic proposition can always be brought down to some particular consequence, in our future practical experience, whether active or passive; the point lying rather in the fact that the experience must be particular, than in the fact that it must be active."

What James was doing was stretching a principle of scientific inquiry to cover thinking generally. The principle of scientific inquiry is the "principle of Peirce." It states that if we want our conception of an object to be meaningful -- or, as Peirce put it, to be "clear" -- then we should limit that conception to the real-world behavior the object will exhibit under all possible conditions. To use one of Peirce's examples, what we mean when we call a substance "hard" is that it will scratch glass, resist bending, and so on. "Hardness" is not an abstract property or invisible essence; it is just the sum total of what all hard things do.

James's idea was to extend this way of understanding scientific concepts to all our beliefs. What makes any belief true? he asked. It is not, he thought, its rational self-sufficiency, its ability to stand up to logical scrutiny. It is that we find that holding the belief leads us into more useful relations with the world. James thought that philosophers had wasted huge amounts of time attempting to derive truths from general first principles, trying to prove or disprove rationally the tenets of various philosophical systems, when all they needed to do was to ask what practical effects our choosing one view rather than another might have.

"What is its cash-value in terms of practical experience?" James thought the philosopher ought to ask of any idea, "and what special difference would come into the world according as it were true or false?" Or as he put it more famously, nine years later, in *Pragmatism*: "The true is the name for whatever proves itself to be good in the way of belief, and good, too, for definite and assignable reasons."

Words like practical and cash-value may make James seem an advocate of materialism and science. But one of his chief purposes in introducing pragmatism into philosophy was to open a window, in what he regarded as an excessively materialistic and scientific age, for faith in God. We needn't ask, he thought, whether the existence of God can be proved; we need only ask what difference believing or disbelieving in God will make in our lives. If we wait for absolute proof that there is or is not a God, we will wait forever. We have to choose whether to believe on other criteria-that is, on pragmatic criteria. For this is, James thought, how we make all our choices. We can never hope for absolute proof of anything. All our decisions are bets on what the universe will do....

Within just a few years of James's lecture, pragmatism became a full-fledged intellectual movement.... In 1872 James was just emerging from a nervous collapse that had lasted almost three years. After a wildly peripatetic education in Europe and America, he had finally graduated from the Harvard Medical School (the only course of study he ever completed) in 1869, at the age of twenty-seven, and immediately fallen into a state of lassitude, depression, and chronic ill health. Whatever the causes of his various symptoms, James seems to have explained them to himself in intellectual terms. He treated his depression as a kind of philosophical problem that might be relieved by coming up with a philosophical solution, and one day in 1870, in his diary, he announced a breakthrough. "...My first act of free will shall be to believe in free will.... Hitherto, when I have felt like taking a free initiative, like daring to act originally, without carefully waiting for contemplation of the external world to determine all for me, suicide seemed the most manly form to put my daring into: now, I will go a step further with my will, not only act with it, but believe as well; believe in my individual reality and creative power." The breakthrough did not prove definitive; James's complaints persisted. But this passage, with its admonition to act on beliefs without waiting for philosophical confirmation of their validity, is the germ of the doctrine James would announce, twenty-six years later, in "The Will to Believe." And it is the essence of his pragmatism.

Holmes underwent his own crisis in a very different setting. In 1861, at the end of his senior year at Harvard, he enlisted in the Union Army (something James seems scarcely to have contemplated), and he served for three years and in some of the bloodiest fighting of the Civil War. Although he later gave speeches in which he glorified the soldier's blind allegiance to duty, Holmes hated war itself. He was seriously wounded three times; the third wound was in the foot, which he hoped would have to be amputated so he could be discharged before his commission was up. That hope was disappointed, but Holmes did emerge from the war purged of illusions. He thought he had paid a high price for the privilege of losing them, and he was careful never to acquire any again.

After his return Holmes attended Harvard Law School and then went into practice with a Boston firm. He also developed an intimate friendship with William James. Their letters were unusually warm and spirited, but their personal relations eventually became strained, and Holmes was always unsympathetic to James's philosophical writings. They seemed to promote, in their spiritual hopefulness, just the sort of sentimental idealism he had rejected. "His wishes led him to turn down the lights so as to give miracle a chance," he complained to a friend after James's death in 1910. Holmes had no high regard for Peirce either;

he thought his genius "overrated." But although Holmes would never have referred to himself as a pragmatist, his twentieth-century disciples have not been wrong to understand his jurisprudence as a form of pragmatism.

In 1870, when he was twenty-nine, Holmes became co-editor of the *American Law Review*, and the first paragraph of the first article he published there gives, in a very early nutshell, the pragmatist premise of his jurisprudence: "It is the merit of the common law that it decides the case first and determines the principle afterwards. Looking at the forms of logic it might be inferred that when you have a minor premise and a conclusion, there must be a major, which you are also prepared then and there to assert. But in fact lawyers, like other men, frequently see well enough how they ought to decide on a given state of facts without being very clear as to the ratio decidendi [the ground of the decision]. Lord Mansfield's often-quoted advice to the business man who was suddenly appointed judge, that he should state his conclusions and not give his reasons, as his judgment would probably be right and the reasons wrong, is not without application to more educated courts."

Holmes's target in these sentences was legal formalism, the theory that the law has an internal logical consistency and consists of general doctrines -- such as "a person shall not use his property in a way that injures the property of another" -- that guide the outcomes of particular cases. Holmes devoted his career as a judge and a jurisprudential thinker to demolishing this view of the law, pointing out, for example, that people use their property legally to injure the property of others all the time, as when they set up a shop with the intention of putting the shop owner down the street out of business.

Holmes's insight into the insufficiency of general principles left him with an obvious question, which is, If general principles don't decide cases, what does? His answer was unveiled in the opening paragraph of *The Common Law* (1881), in what is possibly the most famous sentence in American legal thought: "The life of the law has not been logic; it has been experience." Holmes did not mean that there is no logic in the law. He meant that what guides the direction of the law, from case to case over time, is not immutable reason but changing experience.... Experience, for him, was the name for everything that arises out of the interaction of the human organism with its environment: beliefs, values, intuitions, customs, prejudices-what he called "the felt necessities of the time." Our word for it is culture....

Philosophies and theories and formal methodologies are part of our culture, but they are, in Holmes's view, the dinner jacket and bow tie we instinctively take off when it is time to change the tires. "All the pleasure of life is in general ideas," he wrote to a correspondent in 1899. "But all the use of life is in specific solutions -- which cannot be reached through generalities any more than a picture can be painted by knowing some rules of method. They are reached by insight, tact and specific knowledge."

The one self-proclaimed pragmatist whose writings Holmes admired (and

Holmes was not a man ordinarily given to admiration for the views of other people) was John Dewey. In the final chapter of *Experience and Nature* (1925), the work of the widest philosophical scope among his many books, Dewey praised Holmes as "one of our greatest American philosophers" and went on to quote a long passage from Holmes's essay "Natural Law" (1918)....

Dewey's influence in his own long lifetime -- he was born in 1859, the year of *On the Origin of Species*, and died in 1952, the year of the hydrogen bomb -- touched many fields. He was a psychologist, a philosopher, a political activist, a public intellectual, and a social reformer. But his most lasting contribution was in the field of education, and although pragmatism, once he took it up, underwrote everything Dewey did, it is his work as an educator that shows its consequences most dramatically.

Dewey began his career as an absolute idealist. He was trained at Johns Hopkins . . . by George Sylvester Morris, a neo-Hegelian, and he wrote his first books under the influence of Hegel. His work began turning in a pragmatist direction after he read James's Principles of Psychology in 1890. In 1894 he accepted a position as chair of the philosophy department at the newly founded University of Chicago. In 1896 he established the Laboratory School there, an experiment in progressive education run by the department of pedagogy (of which he was also the chair), and began to write the works on education for which he quickly became famous around the world: *The School and Society* (1899), *The Child and the Curriculum* (1902), *How We Think* (1910), and *Democracy and Education* (1916). The first of these, *The School and Society*, is one of the most influential educational treatises ever written....

Dewey regarded *Democracy and Education*, when it appeared, as the summa of his thought. He believed that philosophers had invented an invidious distinction between knowing and doing, a distinction that had had the intellectually pernicious effect of producing a series of pseudoproblems about the relations between the mind and reality and the socially pernicious effect of elevating a leisure class of speculative thinkers above the world's workers and doers. There was, Dewey thought, no such distinction. Knowing and doing are indivisible aspects of the same process, which is the business of adaptation. We learn, in the progressivist phrase, by doing. We take a piece of acquired knowledge into a concrete situation, and the results we get constitute a new piece of knowledge, which we carry over into our next encounter with the environment. When we try to pin down knowledge by embalming it in a textbook, we cut off thought from experience, and we damage our relations with the world. Knowledge is not a mental copy of a reality external to us; "it is an instrument or organ of successful action."

What is democratic about Dewey's theory is that it conceives of learning as a collaborative activity. Dewey thought of the school as a "miniature community," a kind of training camp for life in a democracy. "The only way to prepare for social life," as he put it, "is to engage in social life," and this emphasis on the associated nature of human existence is crucial to most of what he wrote about politics and social reform. He believed that individual fulfillment could be achieved only through participation in the collective life; for, outside the collectivity no such thing as an individual was possible. "The non-social individual," he wrote in one of his earliest essays, "is an abstraction arrived at by imagining what man would be if all his human qualities were taken away...."

It is common today to speak of a revival of pragmatism, a phenomenon usually dated from the publication of Richard Rorty's *Philosophy and the Mirror of Nature* in 1979. The implication is that . . . pragmatism went into eclipse and that only in the last fifteen years has it re-emerged as a distinctively American style of thought with wide appeal. This notion is not entirely false. Pragmatism after Dewey did go into relative eclipse, and twentieth-century intellectuals have been more likely to identify themselves with other schools of thought -- Marxism, psychoanalysis, existentialism, and structuralism than to think of themselves as pragmatists.

But the notion that pragmatism was eclipsed by other schools of thought in the twentieth century is also a little misleading, and the reason is that it is part of the nature of pragmatism to decline the honor of becoming a "school of thought." Pragmatists have always been wary of the danger that pragmatism will turn into a discipline, just another one of the things people "do." James presented pragmatism, after all, not as a philosophy but as a way of doing philosophy. Pragmatism, in the most basic sense, is about how we think, not what we ought to think....

The threads that lead out of the pragmatist knot and into twentieth-century thought are as various as the threads that lead into it. Pragmatism served as a kind of philosophical tonic for many twentieth-century thinkers whom it would seem beside the point to call pragmatists. One of the most striking effects of the contemporary pragmatist revival is that a whole array of American (and non-American) writers has suddenly been placed in a new shared context. Cornel West, in The *American Evasion of Philosophy* (1990), uses pragmatism to show what people like James, W. E. B. Du Bois, Reinhold Niebuhr, and Lionel Trilling have in common, just as Rorty, in *Philosophy and the Mirror of Nature* and *Consequences of Pragmatism* (1982), uses pragmatism to show what people like Dewey, Martin Heidegger, Ludwig Wittgenstein, and Jacques Derrida have in common, and Richard Poirier, in *Poetry and Pragmatism* (1992), uses it to show what Emerson, Robert Frost, and Gertrude Stein have in common. A complete list of American writers who have acknowledged the stimulus of pragmatism would be varied and long and would include, besides those just named, Wallace Stevens, Learned Hand, Benjamin Cardozo, Kenneth Burke, Sidney Hook, C. Wright Mills, Arthur Schlesinger, Jr., Tom Hayden, and Harold Bloom.

Of the various strands emerging from the pragmatism of James and Dewey, four in particular lead into the cluster of concerns that have helped revive interest in pragmatism. One is the development of theories of cultural pluralism in response to the xenophobia induced by the turn-of-the-century waves of immigration and exacerbated by America's entry into the First World War . . . . Cultural pluralism is the recipe for civil cohesion, and the pragmatic beauty of the formulation is that neither human sameness nor human difference is made to seem essential.

A second consequence of turn-of-the-century pragmatism was the revolution in American law and legal thinking inspired by the writings, and to some extent the personality, of Holmes. In old age -- he was sixty-one when he was appointed to the Supreme Court, in 1902, and he served until he was ninety -- Holmes became a hero to progressive political writers. He was himself a progressive only in a neutral sense. He didn't believe that social and economic reform could do more than shift a few burdens incrementally in one direction or another; he considered economic relations more or less fixed. But he saw no constitutional barrier to legislative attempts to move those burdens, by imposing taxes, passing health and safety regulations, or protecting unions, and this endeared him to progressives who did believe in the powers of reform.

Holmes's belief in society's right to try out new forms of self-regulation followed from his belief, shared by all pragmatists, in the virtues of experimentation. If we learn by doing, we have to keep doing new things, since that is how knowledge progresses or at least adapts. This was the rationale for Holmes's most celebrated opinion as a judge, his dissent in Abrams v. U.S. (1919), in which he rejected state efforts to punish political opinion as a foreclosing of social possibilities. Even the Constitution, he said, "is an experiment, as all life is an experiment. Every year if not every day we have to wager our salvation upon some prophecy based upon imperfect knowledge. While that experiment is part of our system I think that we should be eternally vigilant against attempts to check the expression of opinions that we loathe and believe to be fraught with death...."

A third strand that has recently re-emerged from early pragmatist thought involves the educational philosophy developed around the turn of the century by John Dewey. That philosophy -- the theory that children "learn by doing" -- established itself long ago in the field of early-childhood education, but until the 1980s its relevance to undergraduate education seemed remote. Then, in an essay titled "Toward Pragmatic Liberal Education" in 1995, the historian Bruce A. Kimball argued that trends in undergraduate education since the 1960s reflect a move toward a pragmatic educational philosophy. For a century American higher education was dominated by the model of knowledge that obtains in research universities, where learning is split up among separate scholarly disciplines, or departments; where the emphasis is on "knowledge for its own sake"; where a distinction between "facts" and "values" is rigorously observed; and where education is divorced from practical affairs. Kimball maintained that in smaller liberal arts colleges across the country, educators have been quietly abandoning the research model and have been adopting curricula in which learning is oriented toward values, toward citizenship, toward the recognition of cultural diversity, and toward the Deweyan virtue of "doing." This new model stresses "general education" -- that is, education designed for all students, rather than for future specialists in an academic field of inquiry -- and "liberal education" -- the education of temperament and sensibility....

The final strand connecting turn-of-the-century pragmatism with its late-twentieth-century avatar may seem the most obvious, but it is in fact the oddest. This is the strand that runs through philosophy itself. James and Dewey regarded themselves as philosophers, but it is not hard to see how their dismissal of the traditional problems of philosophy made them seem, to many professional philosophers, enemies of the discipline. Pragmatism is antiformalist; it represents a principle of endless assault on every tendency to erect contingent knowledge into a formal system. To the extent that philosophy is an effort to erect what we know about how we know into a formal system, pragmatism cannot help acting the role of termite-undermining foundations, collapsing distinctions, deflating abstractions, suggesting that the real work of the world is being done somewhere other than in philosophy departments.

In spite of this, James and Dewey not only regarded themselves as philosophers but were, in their day, builders of philosophy departments -- James at Harvard and Dewey at Chicago and then Columbia. Thus there has been, ever since James's lecture "Philosophical Conceptions and Practical Results" in 1898, a tradition of professional pragmatist philosophy, begun by students and colleagues of James and Dewey and running into the present....

As James discovered during his crisis of 1870, pragmatism can encourage us to trust our own judgments, without ever assuming them to be infallible -- to have faith that if we do what is right, the metaphysics will take care of themselves. What pragmatism cannot do, though, is to explain where our judgments come from. The easy answer to that question today is to say that our decisions are determined by the cultural "rules" of the social group we happen to belong to. No doubt the cultural rules explain a great deal of what people do, but different individuals in the same group make different judgments -- if they didn't, there would be nothing that needed explaining -- and in the end, as Holmes concluded, we can't say in any determinate way how we make our choices. They seem to arise, in the end, out of the mysteries of personality, which are a scandal to theory. All we can say is that we seem to have, as naturally associated beings, a powerful social incentive to rationalize and justify the choices we make.

It is sometimes complained that pragmatism is a bootstrap theory -- that it cannot tell us where we should want to go or how we can get there. The answer to this is that theory can never tell us where to go; only we can tell us where to go. Theories are just one of the ways we make sense of our need to get there. We wake up one morning and find ourselves in a new place, and then we build a ladder to explain how we got there. The pragmatist is the person who asks whether this is a good place to be. The nonpragmatist is the person who admires

80

the ladder.

October 1997

Questions:

(1.) Examine your own views about the tension between thought and action. Do you agree with the pragmatists that doers deserve every bit as much respect as thinkers, that practitioners are no less important than theorists? Who was more important to the young United States – George Washington, who fought to secure victory in the American Revolution, or James Madison, who thought to design the new Constitution?

(2.) Oliver Wendell Holmes believed that specific solutions to real-world problems could not be reached by acting according to theory, but only through "insight, tact, and specific knowledge." If Holmes is right, then what is the value of theory? When is theory most useful?

(3.) Why does pragmatism hold such appeal to Americans? What is it about our history and the
formative experiences of our nation that makes us a pragmatic people? As the United States ages, do you think it will become more or less pragmatic about its approaches to both domestic and international issues?

CHAPTER 8

WHERE HAVE ALL THE GREAT MEN GONE?

Richard D. Brown

Were leaders made of "better stuff" during the days of the early republic? In Richard Brown's essay he responds to the question "Where have all the Great Men Gone?" Interestingly, his answer says little about individual character but a lot about the American electoral process. Brown contends that though we do tend to romanticize our early leaders, overall they were quite an exceptional group. Our Founding Fathers were members of what was considered a "natural aristocracy," promoted and recruited by their fellow elites. As demands for more popular participation grew, Brown maintains that the "quality" of our leaders declined. Brown's provocative article asks us to consider if our system is set up to elect the best among us. Further, even if it is not set up to promote the best, is elite recruitment consistent with democratic principles?

There is no clear consensus on what constitutes greatness, nor are there any objective criteria for measuring it—but when we look at holders of high public offices and at the current field of candidates, we know it is missing. Some of our leaders are competent, articulate, engaging, and some are honest and honorable. But greatness is missing.

The leaders of the early republic—George Washington, Thomas Jefferson, John Adams, Benjamin Franklin, Alexander Hamilton, and John Marshall—set the standard for greatness. Since their day only Abraham Lincoln and Franklin D. Roosevelt have attained equivalent stature. Why has mediocrity come to prevail where meritocracy once ruled? Where have all the great men gone?

This question is more complicated than it may first appear, and some will argue that the issues it raises are false and ahistorical, since responses to the question must be subjective. Indeed, some will say that to pose the question is to retreat into romantic mythology where the founders of the republic become the heroic figures of a "golden age." These objections cannot be ignored.

It has been said that a statesman is nothing but a dead politician. From the time we are children we are taught not to speak ill of the dead, and in public rhetoric it is common to elevate them. In our own time admiration for John F. Kennedy exemplifies this phenomenon, and earlier in this century the reputation of the assassinated President William McKinley enjoyed a similar glorification that only gradually ebbed away. Nostalgia distorts historical perceptions, a fact that has nourished revisionist historiography for generations. In fact, revisionism in American historical writing began with the early twentieth-century discovery that the Founding Fathers were flesh-and-blood politicians, and however obvious that "discovery" now appears, it remains a vital corrective to "golden age" thinking.

Yet even admitting all of this, scholars who have closely scrutinized the major leaders of the early republic continue to be enormously impressed. The array of talented and devoted individuals is awesome. In Massachusetts, for instance, John and Samuel Adams, Elbridge Gerry and John Hancock, Robert Treat Paine and James and Joseph Warren, immediately come to mind, as well as a dozen less exalted figures—a James Bowdoin, a Henry Knox, a Benjamin Lincoln, a James Sullivan. We need not agree that they all were truly great, but if we compare them with the present incumbents, the sense of loss and deprivation is overwhelming.

At the end of the eighteenth century as today, political leaders were chiefly drawn from the white male population aged forty to sixty years. Leaving aside questions of wealth and education, Massachusetts in 1790 possessed about thirty thousand such people, the United States as a whole some two-hundred and fifty thousand. Today there are eighty times that number nationwide, twenty million white men aged forty to sixty years. And the total voting population of that age is forty-four million. Considered in light of these figures, the ability of the early republic to generate so many talented officeholders cannot be dismissed as mere patriotic mythology. We are talking about an actual fact.

Biographies cannot provide an explanation. The almost routine emergence of such able leaders was a social phenomenon, and to understand it we must examine the society that produced them. What were the conditions that created this political pattern, and when and why did it recede?

The folklore of politics teaches us that great events produce great men, and we can all think of examples where great events ennobled public figures who had previously and accurately been viewed as undistinguished. In 1932 the journalist Walter Lippmann observed that Franklin D. Roosevelt was "an amiable Boy Scout . . . a pleasant man who, without any important qualifications for the office, would very much like to be President." Unquestionably, the crises of the Depression and World War II elevated Roosevelt's leadership. Had be served during the 1920s, there is no reason to believe his Presidency would be memorable.

Yet this phenomenon is not inevitable. Great events and great challenges produce George McClellans and George Wallaces as well as George Washingtons. No natural law requires societies to assign their most talented members to positions of public trust in times of crises. To understand the nature of how we actually do select our leaders, we must begin by examining the systems of recruiting and advancing public officials within a republican government.

I believe that the United States currently operates a peculiar, debased form of meritocracy, which has five major attributes: first, access to high office is extremely competitive; second, keen personal ambition for power and recognition is necessary to propel people into the competition and keep them there; third, the system calls for a record of experience in public or quasi-public affairs; fourth, it requires visibility through media exposure; finally, what these four elements point to is the fifth characteristic of our system of recruitment and advancement—electioneering performance. The ability to perform in election contests, to go out tirelessly day after day in search of support and to win it from people of diverse characteristics—this is the ultimate criterion.

This system of political advancement operates directly through the electorate and indirectly through elites that recognize the ultimate authority of the ballot box. Because the electorate and the elites are so diverse, electioneering on a national scale or in any large state requires tireless campaigning to persuade people from a multitude of different backgrounds, often with directly conflicting interests, to look with hopeful anticipation on a single person. Chameleonlike, the candidate must appeal to boardroom and back room, fans of symphonies and Super Bowls. From the standpoint of electioneering, our current system is meritocratic, but the attributes that lead to success at the ballot box often seem to assure mediocrity in public office.

It was not always thus. At the outset of the republic, recruitment and advancement operated differently. First of all, the electorate was confined to white, male property-holders who had been schooled in the deferential polities of the colonial era. This was an electorate that expected political leaders to be men of wealth and education, not ordinary people like themselves. Moreover, in choosing candidates, voters were accustomed to supporting men whom they knew face-to-face or through local reputation. If they voted for a stranger, it was usually because that stranger carried the endorsement of a trusted member of the local elite. As far as the electorate was concerned, the role of candidates themselves in seeking office was largely passive.

The key process of nominating candidates was dominated by layers of local, state, and national elites. Candidates were selected by their peers, people who had witnessed them in action for years and who knew first-hand their strengths and weaknesses. Whatever the office in question, relatively homogeneous groups of incumbents and their associates selected candidates from among their own number. While the system was open to new men, and choices required approval at the polls, it had a distinctly, oligarchic flavor. High esteem among the peer group was a prerequisite for major elective offices.

This brief comparison between the present system, where electoral popularity is the ultimate criterion, and the early republic, where peer-group approval was paramount, helps to focus our analysis, but it does not answer the question of the disappearing great men. Though it might be tempting to offer a simple elitist explanation, this would be worse than inadequate; it would be wrong. Historically the records of elite selection processes are replete with instances of incompetence, corruption, and tyranny—and mediocrity. Whether operated by Byrd in Virginia, Daley in Chicago, or Tweed in New York City, the record of oligarchic rule inside the United States, as elsewhere, is not synonymous with meritocracy. The central question then is not techniques of recruitment and advancement per se; it is the values that animate the process.

During the first generation of the republic there was a clear consensus among leading men in all parts of the nation regarding fundamental political values. This consensus was grounded on the classical models that were central to the curricula at all the colonial colleges, from William and Mary in Virginia to Harvard in Massachusetts. Ideals of citizenship and public office were drawn from the history of the Roman republic. First of all, private, personal virtue was a prerequisite to public virtue and hence a requirement for high office. The object of political leadership was to implement the general public good, and in order to perceive and pursue it, leaders must be men of superior wisdom, energy, initiative, and moral stature. The people were not their guides; they were their charges, to be led along paths selected by the leaders. An aristocracy of merit— Jefferson called it a "natural aristocracy"—should rule.

In practical politics this classical model dictated that the man should never seek the office, the office should seek the man. The historical figure of Cincinnatus, who had been called from his plow to lead his people, was the ideal type. In our Revolutionary days, George Washington and Israel Putnam, among others, were presented in this mold.

Anyone familiar with behind-the-scenes politics from 1776 onward knows that these ideals were commonly violated. The launching of the new state and national governments generated a bonanza in vacant offices, and a wave of office seekers rushed in upon them. In the lower echelons of the civilian and military establishments, place seeking was routine. At higher levels the process of recruitment and advancement was much more complicated, and the influence of the new republican idealism on actual practice was far more evident. Patronage connections remained vital, but the meritocratic possibilities of patronage developed a new importance.

The situation is illustrated by the efforts of the Continental Congress to fill its complement of officers for the Army. British colonial tradition dictated that such offices be filled according to principles of venality—that is, personal influence, tempered by some attention to seniority within the ranks of officers. But the Congress broke with tradition, and on May 10, 1776, it formally adopted a policy of "promoting the officers in the continental service according to their merit." Five months later the Congress even repudiated the principle of seniority in favor of merit, recommending to the states that "all the officers to be hereafter appointed, be men of honor and known abilities, without a particular regard to their having before been in service." This recommendation was political dynamite, and even the normally acquiescent General Washington took issue with it, arguing that unless promotions were compatible with seniority, the officer corps would be demoralized. A compromise was finally proposed in which prior rank and merit both had a part, but with the understanding that Congress might deviate from any of its rules "in favour of merit eminently distinguished and generally acknowledged." In the accompanying debate John Adams vigorously rebutted the arguments of Washington and those who counseled in favor of seniority. "I have no fears from the resignation of Officers if junior Officers are preferred to them," Adams declared. "If they have virtue they will continue with us. If not," he concluded, "their resignation will not hurt us." Adams, a key member of the board of war, had been wrestling with the problem for nearly two years and he was convinced that meritocracy could work.

The difficulty of any merit system is how to measure merit. Early republican leaders sought the judgments of informed gentlemen, relying on their discretion as to whether merit was "eminently distinguished and generally acknowledged." Here personal acquaintance—"connections"—was often crucial, and the meritocratic possibilities of patronage were developed.

At the core of the system trust ruled. Assessments of character and abilities were necessarily subjective, so those who selected candidates for civil and military office had to rely on the testimony of their peers. John Adams's correspondence as a member of the board of war illustrates the system's values and the way it worked. To his old law clerk, Adams wrote in August 1776: "I am . . . determined to pursue this Correspondence, until I can obtain a perfect Knowledge of the Characters of our Field Officers." Of one man Adams asserted: "His Genius is equal to any one of his Age. His Education is not inferiour. So far I can Say of my own Knowledge"; but before Adams could recommend promotion, he needed to know more about the candidate's "Morals, his Honour, and his Discretion." On the same day Adams complained in another letter to a colleague that Massachusetts

continues to act, the most odd Surprizing and unaccountable Part, respecting Officers. They have a most wonderful Faculty of finding out Persons for Generals and Colonells of whom no Body ever heard before. Let me beg of you, in Confidence to give me your candid and explicit opinion, of the Massachusetts General and Field Officers, and point out such as have any Education, Erudition, Sentiment, Reflection, Address or other Qualification or Accomplishment excepting Honour and Valour for Officers in high Rank. Who and What is General Fellows? Who and What is General Brickett? . . .

If there are any officers, young or old, among the Massachusetts Forces who have Genius, Spirit, Reflection, Science, Literature, and Breeding, do for the Lands sake, and the Armys sake, and the Province sake let me know their Names, Places of Abodes and Characters.

Adams was a part of a national talent search, and he begged for candid assessments of individuals. The reports he received from political acquaintances in the Northern states reveal the application of meritocratic principles to the process of advancing people according to known connections. From New York a friend of Adams, a lawyer, now serving as a Continental officer, provided him with these ratings of the Massachusetts colonels:

WHITCOMB: has no Trace of an Officer, his Men under no Government
REED: A good Officer not of the most extensive Knowledge but far from being low or despicable . . .
LITTLE: A Midling Officer and of tolerable Genius, not great
SERJEANT: has a pretty good Character but I have no Acquaintance
GLOVER: is said to be a good Officer but am not acquainted
HUTCHINSON: An easy good Man not of great Genius
BALEY: is Nothing
BALDWIN: a Personable Man but not of the first Character
LEARNED: Was a good officer, is old, Superanuated and Resigned
GREATON: An excellent Disciplinarian his Courage has been questioned, but I don't know with what Justice
BOND: I don't know him
PATTERSON: A Good Officer of a liberal Education, ingenious and Sensible.

The key, qualifications are knowledge, "genius," and judgment in addition to the courage and moral character that were prerequisites.

For the highest positions, such as major general, and later for President, much more was wanted. In August 1776 Adams reflected on the essential qualities for the highest of offices. Such a person, Adams believed: "should be possessed of a very extensive Knowledge of Science, and Literature, Men and Things. A Citizen of a free Government, be Should be Master of the Laws and Constitution, least he injure fundamentally those Rights which he professes to defend. He Should have a keen Penetration and a deep Discernment of the Tempers, Natures, and Characters of Men. He Should have an Activity, and Diligence, Superiour to all Fatigue. He should have a Patience and Self Government, Superior to all Flights and Transports of Passion. He Should have a Candour and Moderation, above all Prejudices, and Partialities. His Views should be large enough to comprehend the whole System of the Government and the Army. . . . His Benevolence and Humanity, his Decency, Politeness and Civility, Should ever predominate in his Breast. He should be possessed of a certain . . . order, Method, and Decision, Superior to all Perplexity and Confusion in Business. There is in Such a Character, whenever and wherever it appears, a decisive Energy, which hurries away before it, all Difficulties, and leaves to the World of Mankind no Leisure, or opportunity to do any Thing towards it, but Admire, it." From the perspective of 1776, Adams's idealism was not idle fantasy. Already the Continental Congress and the republic had found one such individual in George Washington.

In order to discern such qualities one could only resort to known men. Speaking of the selection of officers in October 1775, Adams remarked that "Men of Honour cannot appoint Gentlemen whom they don't know. . . . Nor can they pay a Regard to any Recommendation of Strangers, to the Exclusion of Persons whom they know." Personal knowledge and the recommendations of acquaintances—personal connections—were crucial. Traditionally these were the mechanisms of patronage, where friends and relatives sponsored each other's promotion, with merit no more than a secondary consideration. In the Revolutionary republic at its best, however, the new idealism transformed old, quasi- oligarchic practices into a screen for talent, wisdom, and character.

There was a genuine convergence between the real and the ideal, but it should not be overdrawn. In staffing Massachusetts's officer corps, the champions of meritocracy faced formidable obstacles that were intrinsic to a representative government. The policy of Massachusetts, it was acidly remarked, was "to thrust into Notice Men, whom Nature design'd for Obscurity." Though mediocrity had no defenders, there were real pressures to recruit and advance men of mediocre abilities and, as a corollary, some willingness to discourage the best qualified from public service.

John Adams grasped the problem immediately. In a popular representative government, the elitism that was inseparably connected to the development of a natural aristocracy was suspect: "Knowledge is among the most essential Foundations of Liberty. But is there not a Jealousy or an Envy taking Place among the Multitude of Men of Learning, and, a wish to exclude them from the public Councils and from military Command? I could mention many Phenomena, in various Parts of these States, which indicate such a growing Disposition. To what Cause Shall I attribute the Surprizing Conduct of the Massachusetts Bay? How has it happened that such an illiterate Group of General and Field Officers, have been thrust into public View, by that Commonwealth which . . . ought to have set an Example to her sisters, by sending into the Field her best Men. Men of the most Genius Learning, Reflection, and Address. Instead of this, every Man you send into the Army as a General or a Collonell exhibits a Character, which nobody ever heard of before, or an awkward, illiterate, ill bred Man . . . there is not a Single Man among all our Collonells that I dare to recommend for a General Officer, except Knox and Porter." Adams and his peers associated learning and largeness of view with merit, and the fact that these qualities also correlated substantially with wealth and social status seemed natural and appropriate to them.

But ordinary people were not fully in agreement. John Adams wrote in alarm: "I fear we shall find that popular Elections are not oftener determined, upon pure Principles of Merit, Virtue, and public Spirit, than the Nominations of a Court, if We don't take Care. I fear there is an infinity of Corruption in our Elections already crept in. All Kinds of Favour, Intrigue and Partiality in Elections are as real, Corruption in my Mind, as Treats and Bribes. . . . A Sober, conscientious Habit, of electing for the public good alone must be introduced, and every Appearance of Interest, Favour, and Partiality, reprobated, or you will very soon make wise and honest Men wish for Monarchy again, nay you will make them introduce it into America." Long before the emergence of the Federalist movement, Adams foresaw the tensions between elite political expectations and government based on popular elections.

Actually, Gordon S. Wood, the leading authority on the effort to create the Constitution of 1787, believes that one of its central objectives was to screen out the direct influence of the people from the government, enabling the elites to select from among their own number the people they believed were best qualified to guide the United States. The provisions of the Constitution prescribing the selection of the principal public officials clearly limited the impact of popular elections. The President was to be chosen by an Electoral College, and failing a majority there, by the House of Representatives. The members of the United States Senate were to be elected by the individual state legislatures. The only popularly elected officers would be members of the House of Representatives, but since their constituencies were so large (at least forty thousand people), it was believed that only prominent men of proven abilities would possess the visibility and wide acquaintance necessary for election.

The conviction that men of merit according to upper-class standards must dominate public office was a consistent theme in the Federalist administrations of Washington and Adams, but the election of 1800 and the ensuing party competition between Jeffersonians and Federalists pointed in a new direction. After Jefferson took office, even the majority of Federalists were prepared to give the people what they wanted, tailoring policy to popular wishes instead of to abstract principles of the public good. While it is hard to fix a precise date for the demise of the system of political recruitment and advancement that produced so many great men, it was weakening in the early decades of the new century, and in the presidential election of 1828 its utter defeat is evident.

As President, John Quincy Adams was a political anachronism. His election in 1824 was the only case where the electoral process set up in 1787 to assure the best choice in case of deadlock had actually been employed. When no one commanded a majority in the Electoral College, the selection of the

President fell to the House of Representatives. Here his fellow candidate Henry Clay decided that Adams would make a better President than Andrew Jackson, who had won a plurality of popular votes. Whatever Clay's motives, by following this course he directly repudiated the popular vote as well as the instructions of his own Kentucky legislature. The system of elite selection worked, for Adams was indeed superbly qualified for the highest office according to the classical republican canons of education, experience, intelligence, energy, and moral stature. But he lacked popularity and the willingness to seek it. In 1828 he and the meritocratic system he symbolized were defeated.

John Quincy Adams saw clearly what was going on. In his memoirs he confided: "Electioneering for the Presidency has spread its contagion to the President himself. . . . One of the most remarkable peculiarities of the present time is that the principal leaders of the political parties are travelling about the country from State to State, and holding forth, like Methodist preachers, hour after hour, to assembled multitudes, under the broad canopy of heaven." Adams would not lift a finger to pursue reelection. He ignored his own party's pleas for help and even refused to state that he wished to be elected. Like a caricature of the classical ideal, he stood for office in silence.

Meanwhile, professional politicians flocked to Andrew Jackson because his military reputation made him famous and popular. Jackson's career lent itself to magnification, and strategists organized parties, parades, and house-to-house canvassing to turn out the Jackson vote in 1828 on behalf of a common man's crusade. Though Andrew Jackson was a person of unusual ability and genuine achievement, he was elected because he appeared to symbolize popular feelings. In 1840, when the Whigs successfully ran the aged and obscure William Henry Harrison as a Jackson look-alike in the "hard-cider," "log-cabin," "Tippecanoe and Tyler too" campaign, the absolute corruption of the selection process was evident. Mediocrity was more popular than meritocracy, and henceforth it would be qualities associated with electioneering success that would determine recruitment and advancement.

Elites still selected candidates in party caucuses and conventions, but they measured their choices against popular preferences and party loyalty. In an age when sentiment was supplanting reason in religion and the arts, when egalitarianism was destroying the legitimacy of natural as well as hereditary aristocracy, the values embodied in the classical republican ideal lost out in the race for popularity. During the Civil War the Boston brahmin historian Francis Parkman probed the fundamental issues: "Our ship is among breakers, and we look about us for a pilot. An endangered nation seeks a leader worthy of itself. . . . In a struggle less momentous it found such leaders. . . . Out of three millions, America found a Washington, an Adams, a Franklin, a Jefferson, a Hamilton; out of twenty millions she now finds none whose stature can compare with these. She is strong in multitudes, swarming with brave men, instinct with eager patriotism. But she fails in that which multitudes cannot supply, those master minds, the lack of which the vastest aggregate of mediocrity can never fill. . . . Where are they? Why is mediocrity in our high places, and the race of our statesmen so dwindled? . . . The people have demanded equality, not superiority, and they have had it: men of the people, that is to say, men in no way raised above the ordinary level of humanity. In degrading its high offices, the nation has weakened and degraded itself."

Ironically, these words were written just as the nation was about to discover the greatness of Abraham Lincoln. Yet the fact of Lincoln's ultimate stature does not diminish the cogency of Parkman's analysis. Lincoln was in fact elected as the common man incarnate. The fact that he subsequently displayed the superior qualities of wisdom, rectitude, and courage was accidental. His immediate predecessors in the highest office, Buchanan, Pierce, Fillmore, and Taylor, like his immediate successors, Johnson, Grant, Hayes, and Garfield, testify that the remarkable qualities Lincoln possessed were not requirements for nomination or election.

Today's political system remains dynamic, and it has departed from that of the nineteenth century in a number of important ways. Senators are now elected directly by the voters. Primary elections for state and national offices have partially supplanted party conventions, and candidates appeal to voters directly through radio and television. Yet these developments represent logical extensions of the popular, egalitarian spirit that animated the nineteenth century.

As a result we elect companionable-seeming people who cannot appear aloof, and who are doomed if they seem arrogant or learned. One observer of the 1976 presidential campaign noted that after Jimmy Carter was criticized for the "lack of a self-deprecating humor, for several days he worked humorous remarks about himself into his public appearances." As a candidate, Nixon had labored hard in the same vineyard and even took humor lessons from Bob Hope. For if a candidate possesses qualities that would truly set him off as superior, they must be concealed, since they excite fear and jealousy.

Overall we are more comfortable with people not much different from ourselves. Sen. Roman L. Hruska elevated this observation to a statement of principle in defending President Nixon's nomination of G. Harrold Carswell for the Supreme Court in 1970. Hruska said that he would support Carswell "even if he were mediocre," since "there are a lot of mediocre judges and people and lawyers, and they are entitled to a little representation, aren't they?" Hruska's only error lies in supposing that mediocrity is not already well represented in the high councils of the nation.

Hruska's statement is embarrassing because normally we do not like to admit our suspicion of superiority. In the end, however, we regularly elect plausible, supple politicians who have the patience for endless campaigning and who are appealing rather than admirable.

Still, greatness is not absolutely ruled out. At special historical moments a highest common denominator may be discovered and, as with Lincoln and Roosevelt, greatness may luckily emerge. But greatness, of course, is an exceptional phenomenon; even under the best conditions the odds must always be against it. By selecting leaders as we do, we lengthen those odds dramatically. In order to better our chances, a revolution in our system of recruiting and selecting leaders would be required, as well as a revolution in values. We would have to admit that the people, who glimpse candidates only momentarily from a distance, and through the filters of the media, do not have the capacity to judge who is fit for office. We would have to reject the democratic egalitarian ethos under which our political system has been operating for over a century.

I do not advise revolution. The great men who led in founding our republic would offer the same counsel. After all, they made the Revolution for the sake of liberty through law, and they created the Constitution because history had taught them it was dangerous to rely on the individual merit or virtue of rulers. They placed their faith in constitutional government, arranging power so as to rely on laws, not men. They believed that, in the long run, this gave the best hope for freedom. Their greatest fear was not the mediocrity and inadequacy of leaders, it was the apathy, ignorance, and petty selfishness of the people. When public morals became corrupt, they warned, liberty would languish.

Perhaps their warning is relevant for our own time. Our longing for great men and women to lead us out of the wilderness is, in classical republican terms, a sign of lassitude, of the corruption that encourages demagogues and leads to tyranny. Informed by history, we should understand that the circumstances that led to the sparkling era when personal greatness and high public office coincided were unique, and exceptional. To expect greatness in public office, to anticipate a new meritocracy that can solve our problems, is a fantasy. The public interest and the safety of free government are better served by an alert, informed citizenry seeking to promote the common good. Whether that, too, is fantasy, only time will tell.

February 1984

QUESTIONS

1. Are some people more fit to lead and to rule than others? Is there a natural aristocracy?

2. Is our allegiance to political parties a thing of the past? Is there a reform that would lessen the influence of interest groups and strengthen party competition?

3. Can highly principled individuals win elections? In the process of building electoral coalitions can politicians avoid the middle-of-the road? Give examples.

CHAPTER 9

"IMPEACHMENT AFTERMATH: WILLIAM JEFFERSON CLINTON, ANDREW JOHNSON, AND THE JUDGEMENT OF HISTORY"

Bernard A Weisberger.

President William Jefferson Clinton is only the second president to be impeached by the House of Representatives and acquitted by the Senate. The first chief executive to meet with this fate was Abraham Lincoln's successor, Andrew Johnson, who governed during Reconstruction. Bernard A. Weisberger briefly recounts the circumstances of Johnson's impeachment and acquittal and then sums up the judgment history has reached concerning both Johnson and his political foes. The political passions of today, notes Weisberger, often give way to more measured conclusions. This realization is particularly important given the Framers' suspicions of mass democracy, their emphasis on deliberative governance, and the very high bar they set for removing a president from office: "treason, bribery, or other high crimes and misdemeanors." In light of this, Weisberger offers some thoughts about what history is likely to make of Clinton's misdeeds and the actions of his adversaries.

When the 105th Congress took a pre-election recess last October, the House of Representatives had already made itself a place in the record books by resolving, for the second time in a quarter of a century and only the third in the nation's experience, to hold hearings on the possible impeachment and trial of a President.

I was reluctant to add to the millions of words already saturating the media. By now any reasonably conscious American should know plenty, even about such unintimate matters as the Constitution's definition of impeachable crimes and the 1868 case of Andrew Johnson. Can any further and nonredundant historical framework be supplied?

I make the answer a tentative yes if we think in terms of aftermath. Let us start with a statement and a question. The statement is this: There are those who argue that Clinton's own behavior brought on the crisis and raises constitutional issues worthy of examination; and there are those who see him as essentially the victim of a vendetta by partisan opponents. The question is: Which view is likely to be the judgment of history? On that the Johnson story is potentially instructive.

To get the core facts into as brief a compass as possible, Johnson was an accidental President in more ways than one. He was a rarity, a Southern Democrat -- a senator from Tennessee in 1861 -- who opposed secession and refused to follow his state out of the Union. In 1864, in order to woo Northern and Western Democrats, the Republicans put him on the ticket as Lincoln's running mate. But Johnson remained basically a Democrat, and Booth's bullet put him in the White House in April 1865, confronting a Republican Congress -- which, however, was not slated to meet until December.

In the interim Johnson took charge of Reconstruction. He followed a proposed Lincoln plan of allowing a state to re-enter the Union, provided that 10 percent of its 1860 voters sign an oath of loyalty; that it ratify the Thirteenth Amendment, ending slavery; and that it repudiate its ordinance of secession and debts incurred under the Confederacy. By year's end all the seceded states had done so. Not surprisingly, their voters then elected governors and congressmen who had been Confederate heroes and state lawmakers who enacted black codes, which regulated the behavior and opportunities of the emancipated blacks so stringently that while not precisely returned to slavery, they were left disenfranchised and far from free.

It was not surprising either that these developments did not sit well with a Northern public that had just lost more than 350,000 of its sons in a war against what was perceived as a Southern oligarchy bent on demeaning and destroying free labor and all the educational and industrial progress that went with it. Nor did they please a Congress unwilling to be shut out of the Reconstruction process. When that body reconvened, its Republican majority was fairly well united behind the idea of giving the freedmen more protection and some basic civil rights through a number of measures, including the Fourteenth Amendment. Some Radical Republicans, such as Thaddeus Stevens and Charles Sumner, hoped to go even further and reorganize Southern society by redistributing power downward to a new class of united blacks and whites whose votes would create a Republican South.

Rather than cultivate more moderate Republicans and soothe war-inflamed feelings, Johnson met the enemy head-on. Born in poverty, self-educated, hot-tempered, and used to backwoods stump oratory, he toured the country during the 1866 congressional election campaign, encouraging the South to reject the Fourteenth Amendment and denouncing Stevens and Sumner by name as traitors and comparing them to Judas Iscariot. A huge backlash swept vetoproof Republican majorities into office in the House and Senate, and in both chambers leadership fell to the Radicals.

The new Congress met in March of 1867 and tied Johnson hand and foot. It tore up his Reconstruction plan and imposed a far more exacting one on Sumner-and-Stevens-like terms. Until the South accepted it, the region would be under military control. But the President was Commander in chief, so in order to deprive Johnson of any voice in the occupation, Congress decreed that it would give orders directly to Army commanders through the Secretary of War, who happened to be Edwin M. Stanton, a Lincoln-cabinet holdover who thoroughly agreed with the Radicals. To prevent Johnson from replacing Stanton, the Tenure of Office Act was passed, requiring Senate approval to discharge presidential appointees it had previously confirmed. Johnson fired Stanton anyway, claiming that Congress was unconstitutionally violating the separation of powers, a position upheld by the Supreme Court in a case decided many years later. But Stanton's removal in February of 1868 gave Radicals in the House the chance to impeach an already helpless Johnson, who, by the time of the Senate trial, would have less than a year left in office. His violation of the Tenure of Office Act became the key "high crime and misdemeanor" in eleven charges, including contempt of Congress. The trial lasted from March through May and ended with a 35-19 vote for conviction, one short of the two-thirds necessary, thanks to seven moderate Republicans who broke ranks and voted in Johnson's favor.

So much for narration. What about that verdict of history? After his stormy Presidency, Johnson caught a lucky wave. For a combination of reasons, Reconstruction ended within eight years of his departure from the White House, and a long period of anti-Reconstruction reaction then set in and generated a historical consensus far kinder to the South. The Confederates had fought honorably for their view of the Constitution, surrendered honorably, and honorably accepted the defeat of secession and slavery. Vindictive Radicals, however, with a moderate and conciliatory Lincoln out of the way, had insisted on crushing the defeated "rebels" and saddling them by force with corrupt and thieving state governments run by white "carpetbaggers" and ignorant, easily manipulated blacks. Andrew Johnson's heroic efforts to turn the tide had earned him the venom that resulted in the trumped-up charges. His one-vote "victory" had saved the Constitution from being perverted and turned into a system of parliamentary supremacy. The brave seven Republicans who voted not to convict him thereafter had suffered the destruction of their political careers and reputations. The most vivid written expression of these legends, Claude G. Bowers's *The Tragic Era*, a kind of *Birth of a Nation* in print, appeared in 1929. Two well-received Johnson biographies of the same era reflect the viewpoint in their titles: Lloyd Paul Stryker's *Andrew Johnson: A Study in Courage* (1929) and George Fort Milton's *The Age of Hate: Andrew Johnson and the Radicals* (1930). They were still recommended reading in graduate schools twenty years later, and one of John F. Kennedy's *Profiles in Courage*, which won the Pulitzer Prize in 1957, was of Kansas's senator Edmund G. Ross, the defecting Republican whose vote finally tipped the scales Johnson's way.

Then came the 1960s, since when historians, white and black, have taken a far more accurate, fair, and nuanced view of Reconstruction. Space does not allow me to recapitulate it, but basically it is less racist, less elitist, and more willing to weigh the accomplishments and failings of Reconstruction state governments in context and to acknowledge the hate and violence that were directed against them. The best summary is Eric Foner's 1988 *Reconstruction: America's Unfinished Revolution, 1863-1877.*

And how has Johnson fared since then? Well, he has not been reconverted into the drunken brute of Radical propaganda; neither is he, for recent biographers, a valiant victim (as portrayed by Van Heflin in a 1942 film, *Tennessee Johnson*). Eric L. McKitrick's *Andrew Johnson and Reconstruction* (1960) was groundbreaking, and Albert Castel's *The Presidency of Andrew Johnson* synthesizes fresh studies up to 1979. By the light of most current scholarship, Johnson was a small man who could not rise to a great opportunity for leadership. Far from following Lincoln's lead, he was entirely lacking in the vision, political sensitivity, and willingness to compromise that had guided and would have continued to shape Lincoln's presidential course. Johnson built no bridges to Congress and made enemies at every step of his career. Except for supporting free homesteads and education, he had no notable pre-war track record. He had not opposed slavery so much as the power of rich slaveholders. As President he hated the idea of giving blacks the vote and publicly proclaimed that "left to their own devices," they showed "a constant tendency to lapse into barbarism." In defiance of the trend of his time, he was a States' Rights Jacksonian Democrat on all issues save secession. That he was excessively hounded by the Radicals is clear. That he more or less invited the situation is equally the truth.

What does this tell you about what our grandchildren are likely to read about the Clinton case? It is hard to visualize a future cultural climate that could turn him into a persecuted hero. But it is possible that changed attitudes toward his generation and its moral perspectives may encourage an assessment of his failings, his successes, and his enemies that will result in a positive portrait. There is, after all, hardly any President repudiated in his own time -- Harding comes to mind -- who lacks some historical defender. Clinton could of course be a negative exception, but elapsed time generally tends to bring on kinder judgments, though the rule isn't infallible.

February 1999

Questions:

(1.) Examine your own views about the constitutional process of removing a president. Do you

   share the Framers' skeptical view of human nature and their suspicion of the passions of the masses? Is it not difficult enough – or too difficult – to remove a president, or just about right?

(2.) The Johnson and Clinton impeachment cases seem to have had nearly as much to do with the personal failings of these two presidents as with their constitutional transgressions. Should presidents be personal role models as well as political leaders?

(3.) How do you think history will evaluate Clinton's impeachment and acquittal fifty years from now? Will he fare better or worse than at present?

98

CHAPTER 10

"WHEN THE LAWS WERE SILENT"

William H Rehnquist.

After the Japanese attack at Pearl Harbor, tens of thousands of Americans with Japanese ancestry were taken from their homes and forcibly relocated to internment camps. Was this policy an unpleasant wartime necessity, or was it a fundamental violation of civil liberties? Supreme Court Chief Justice William H. Rehnquist examines the Supreme Court's evolving handling of this matter in three court cases from 1942 through late 1944. Rehnquist notes that the Court traditionally has deferred to the other branches of government during wartime, and that the Court waited until later in the war to tackle the most difficult legal questions associated with the internment of Japanese-Americans. In the future, Rehnquist states, the Court is likely to scrutinize more closely such wartime decisions that affect the civil liberties of American citizens.

The entire nation was stunned by the Japanese attack on Pearl Harbor on December 7, 1941, but it seemed much closer to home on the West Coast than elsewhere on the mainland. Residents became fearful of ethnic Japanese among them. Japanese immigrants had begun to settle on the West Coast shortly before the turn of the century and had not been assimilated into the rest of the population. Under the Naturalization Act of 1790, those who had emigrated from Japan were not able to become citizens; they were prohibited by law from owning land and were socially segregated in many ways. The first generation of Japanese immigrants, the issei, therefore remained aliens. But their children, the nisei, having been born in the United States, were citizens from birth. Californians particularly, including public officials—Gov. Culbert Olson, State Attorney General Earl Warren, and the mayor of Los Angeles, Fletcher Bowron—began to call for "relocation" to the interior of the country of persons of Japanese ancestry. At the outbreak of the war the military established the Western Defense Command, which included the coastal portions of California, Oregon, and Washington. Gen. John DeWitt, its senior officer, at first resisted the clamor to remove the Japanese. But state and local public officials were adamant, and they were supported by their states' congressional delegations. The chorus became more insistent when the Roberts Commission released its report in late January 1942.

On December 18, 1941, President Roosevelt had appointed a body chaired by Owen J. Roberts, an Associate Justice of the Supreme Court, "to ascertain and report the facts relating to the attack made by Japanese armed forces upon the territory of Hawaii on December 7, 1941." The commission met first in Washington and then went to Hawaii, where the members heard numerous witnesses. The commission found that there had been highly organized espionage in Hawaii: "It has been discovered that the Japanese consul sent to and received from Tokyo in his own and other names many messages on commercial radio circuits. This activity greatly increased towards December 7,1941.... [The Japanese] knew from maps which they had obtained, the exact location of vital air fields, hangars, and other structures. They also knew accurately where certain important naval vessels would be berthed. Their fliers had the most detailed maps, courses, and bearings, so that each could attack a given vessel or field. Each seems to have been given a specified mission."

In February 1942 a Japanese submarine shelled oil installations near Santa Barbara. The pressure built for forced evacuation. Attorney General Francis Biddle, Secretary of War Henry L. Stimson, and Assistant Secretary of War John J. McCloy were the decision-makers for the two concerned departments. None of them favored relocation at first, but eventually Stimson and McCloy changed their minds in the course of often heated discussions among themselves and their subordinates. Final approval of course rested with the President. On February 11,1942, McCloy asked Stimson to find out if Roosevelt was willing to authorize the removal of the nisei as well as the issei. Stimson asked to see the President but was told FDR was too busy; a phone call would have to do. "I took up with him the West Coast matter first," Stimson wrote in his diary, "and told him the situation and fortunately found he was very vigorous about it and told me to go ahead on the line that I had myself thought the best."

Then, Stimson wrote in his 1947 memoirs, "mindful of its duty to be prepared for any emergency, the War Department ordered the evacuation of more than a hundred thousand persons of Japanese origin from strategic areas on the west coast. This decision was widely criticized as an unconstitutional invasion of the rights of individuals many of whom were American citizens, but it was eventually approved by the Supreme Court as a legitimate exercise of the war powers of the President. What critics ignored was the situation that led to the evacuation. Japanese raids on the west coast seemed not only possible but probable in the first months of the war, and it was quite impossible to be sure that the raiders would not receive important help from individuals of Japanese origin."

Biddle, who alone among the high administration officials involved opposed the evacuation, described the situation in these words: "Apparently, the War Department's course of action had been tentatively charted by Mr. McCloy and Colonel Karl Robin Bendetsen of the General Staff in the first ten days of February. General DeWitt's final recommendation to evacuate was completed on February 13, and forwarded to Washington with a covering letter the next day. Mr. Stimson and Mr. McCloy did not, however, wait for this report, which contained the 'finding' on which their 'military necessity' argument to the President was based, but obtained their authority before the recommendation was received. On February 11 the President told the War Department to prepare a plan for wholesale evacuation, specifically including citizens. It was dictated, he concluded, by military necessity, and added, 'Be as reasonable as you can.' After the conference the Assistant Secretary reported to Bendetsen: 'We have carte blanche to do what we want as far as the President is concerned.'" Biddle speculated on Roosevelt's feelings about the matter: "I do not think he was much concerned with the gravity or implications of this step. He was never theoretical about things. What must be done to defend the country must be done." Biddle concluded with a remarkably perceptive observation: "Nor do I think that the constitutional difficulty plagued him-the Constitution has never greatly bothered any wartime President. That was a question of law, which ultimately the Supreme Court must decide. And meanwhile—probably a long meanwhile—we must get on with the war."

Executive Order 9066, authorizing the removal of the ethnic Japanese from the West Coast, was signed by Roosevelt on February 19. Several weeks later Congress passed a law imposing criminal penalties for violations of the order or regulations that might be issued to implement it. First a curfew was imposed on the ethnic Japanese, then they were required to report to relocation centers, and finally they were taken to camps in the interior of California and in the mountain states. There was no physical brutality, but there were certainly severe hardships: removal from the place where one lived, often the forced sale of houses and businesses, and harsh living conditions in the Spartan quarters of the internment centers. As the war progressed, some restrictions were relaxed. Nisei volunteers made up the 442d Combat Team, which fought bravely in Italy against the Germans. Other internees were issued work permits that allowed them to leave the camp. Finally, most of those who were still interned were released by the beginning of 1945, as a result of the third Supreme Court decision in which the relocation policy was challenged.

Gordon Hirabayashi was born near Seattle to issei parents in 1918, and by 1942 he was a senior at the University of Washington. In May 1942 he disobeyed the curfew requirement imposed by military authorities pursuant to the President's Executive Order, and seven days later he failed to report to register for evacuation. He was indicted and convicted in a federal court in Seattle on two counts of misdemeanor and sentenced to imprisonment for three months on each. He contended that the orders he was charged with violating were unconstitutional, but the federal judge in Seattle ruled against him. Fred Korematsu, born in the United States to issei parents, was convicted of remaining in San Leandro, California, in violation of a military exclusion order applicable to him. The federal court in San Francisco overruled his claim that the order in question was unconstitutional, suspended his sentence, and placed him on probation for five years.

The cases were argued together before the U.S. Court of Appeals for the Ninth Circuit in San Francisco, which has jurisdiction over the Far Western part of the United States. Because of procedural variations, they reached the Supreme Court at different times. The case of Hirabayashi was sent directly there by the court of appeals and was argued in May 1943....

The Japanese-Americans were represented in the Supreme Court by able counsel, including Edwin Borchard, William Draper Lewis, Brien McMahon, and Osmond K. Fraenkel. Their basic contention was that the President's Executive Order was unconstitutional because it proceeded on the basis that an entire racial group was disloyal, rather than being based on any individual determinations of disloyalty. Briefs supporting these petitioners were filed by the American Civil Liberties Union, the Northern California branch of the American Civil Liberties Union, and the JapaneseAmerican Citizens League.

The government in its brief recited in great detail the calamitous military events of the early days of the war-these ranged from the Pearl Harbor raid to the fall of the British stronghold of Singapore-which it thought justified the orders now being challenged, and went on to catalogue the "concentration of war facilities and installations on the West Coast [that] made it an area of special military concern at any time and especially after the sensational Japanese successes."

The attorneys general of Washington, Oregon, and California filed a brief in support of the government that pointed out that "for the first seven months little occurred to reduce the fear of attack.... On June 3, 1942, Dutch Harbor, Alaska, was attacked by carrier-based planes. On June 7, 1942, the Japanese invaded continental North America by occupying the Islands of Attu and Kiska in the Aleutian group. There was an increasing indication that the enemy had knowledge of our patrols and naval dispositions, for ships leaving west coast ports were being intercepted and attacked regularly by enemy submarines." Following the oral argument and conference in the Hirabayashi case, Chief Justice Stone assigned the task of writing the Court's opinion to himself. He first greatly narrowed the scope of the opinion by deciding that the Court need pass only on the validity of the curfew requirement and not on the requirement that Hirabayashi report to a relocation center. Hirabayashi had been convicted of both offenses, but his sentences were to run "concurrently"—that is, he would serve only three months in prison even though he had been sentenced to serve three months on each of two different charges. Under established law at that time, if the conviction on one count was upheld, the Court would disregard the conviction on the second count, since it essentially made no difference in the amount of time the defendant would spend in prison. In this case it meant that the Court had to tackle only the easier question of whether a curfew might be imposed, rather than the more difficult one of whether Hirabayashi could be sent to an internment camp.

Stone's task in writing the opinion was not an easy one, because several of his colleagues insisted that there be little or no opportunity to challenge the order later, while Justices Douglas, Murphy, and Rutledge wanted explicitly to leave open that possibility. Indeed, Murphy circulated a draft of a caustic dissent that chastised the Court for approving a program that "utterly subverts" individual rights in war. Douglas circulated a concurrence in which he indicated his view that at some point a person interned under the program should have an opportunity to prove his loyalty. Murphy finally turned his draft dissent into a concurrence but said in it that he thought the program "goes to the very brink of constitutional power." Rutledge also filed a brief concurrence.

Stone's opinion for the Court borrowed a definition of the government's war power from a statement made by Charles Evans Hughes—not while he was a member of the Court but in an article in the American Bar Association Journal: The war power of the national government is "the power to wage war successfully," and it was "not for any court to sit in review of the wisdom of their [the Executive's or Congress's] actions, or to substitute its judgment for theirs." If the Court could say there was a rational basis for the military decision, it would be sustained.

Stone's opinion then adduced the facts most of which had been set forth in the government's brief—that showed the threat by the Japanese Navy to the Pacific Coast immediately after the Pearl Harbor bombing. It went on to say: "Whatever views we may entertain regarding the loyalty to this country of the citizens of Japanese ancestry, we cannot reject as unfounded the judgment of the military authorities and of Congress that there were disloyal members of that population, whose number and strength could not be precisely and quickly ascertained. We cannot say that the war-making branches of the Government did not have ground for believing that in a critical hour such persons could not readily be isolated and separately dealt with, and constituted a menace to the national defense and safety, which demanded that prompt and adequate measures be taken to guard against it."

The Court, of course, had to respond to the charge that distinctions based on race alone were not permitted under the Constitution: "Distinctions between citizens solely because of their ancestry are by their very nature odious to a free people whose institutions are founded upon the doctrine of equality.... We may assume that these considerations would be controlling here were it not for the fact that the danger of espionage and sabotage, in time of war and of threatened invasion, calls upon the military authorities to scrutinize every relevant fact bearing on the loyalty of populations in the danger areas. . . . The fact alone that the attack on our shores was threatened by Japan rather than another enemy power set these citizens apart from others who have no particular associations with Japan." Stone's opinion upholding the curfew was joined by five of his colleagues. Douglas, Murphy, and Rutledge, while voting to uphold the curfew, wrote separately.

Korematsu's case did not come on for argument until October 1944. Here the Court was required to confront not merely the curfew but the far more draconian relocation requirement. The Court upheld relocation, in an opinion by Justice Black, basing its reasoning largely on the earlier decision. This time, however, there were separate dissents by Justices Roberts, Murphy, and Jackson. The flavor of Black's opinion is caught in its concluding passage: "To cast this case into outlines of racial prejudice, without reference to the real military dangers which were presented, merely confuses the issue. Korematsu was not excluded from the Military Area because of hostility to him or his race. He was excluded because we are at war with the Japanese Empire, because the properly constituted military authorities feared an invasion of our West Coast and felt constrained to take proper security measures, because they decided that the military urgency of the situation demanded that all citizens of Japanese ancestry be segregated from the West Coast temporarily. . . . There was evidence of disloyalty on the part of some, the military authorities considered that the need for action was great, and time was short. We cannot-by availing ourselves of the calm perspective of hindsight-now say that at that time these actions were unjustified."

Murphy criticized the military for lumping together with a disloyal few of Japanese ancestry all the others against whom there had been no such showing. Jackson said that the Court was simply in no position to evaluate the government's claim of military necessity: "In the very nature of things, military decisions are not susceptible of intelligent judicial appraisal. They do not pretend to rest on evidence, but are made on information that often would not be admissible and on assumptions that could not be proved.... Hence courts can never have any real alternative to accepting the mere declaration of the authority that issued the order that it was reasonably necessary from a military viewpoint."

But in the case of Endo, argued and decided at the same time as Korematsu, the Court reached quite a different result. Mitsuye Endo had submitted to an evacuation order and been removed first to the Tule Lake Relocation Center in the Cascade Mountains just south of the California-Oregon border and then to another relocation center in Utah. She sued out a writ of habeas corpus, claiming that she was a loyal citizen against whom no charge had been made and that she was therefore entitled to her relief. The government agreed that she was a loyal citizen and not charged with any offense. The Court decided that under these circumstances Endo was entitled to be released from confinement. The presidential order and the act of Congress confirming it spoke of evacuation from a military zone but said nothing of detention after the evacuation. While the initial evacuation had been justified in terms of the defense facilities on the West Coast, the detention of a loyal person of Japanese ancestry after the evacuation had taken place was not reasonably necessary to prevent sabotage or espionage. Two members of the Court wrote separately, but all agreed with the result.

Although the Court based its reasoning in Endo on the provisions of the act of Congress and the Executive Order, and therefore Congress and the President would have been free to change those to provide for detention, the Court's opinion strongly hinted at constitutional difficulties if that were to be done. And, it should be noted, the military position of the United States was much more favorable in the fall of 1944 than it had been in the spring of 1942. In the Pacific the U.S. Navy won the Battle of Leyte Gulf in October, and American forces were moving steadily closer to the Japanese homeland. There was neither a military need nor a public demand for further restrictions on Americans of Japanese descent, and the entire program was promptly terminated only two weeks after the decision in the Endo case.

There is a certain disingenuousness in this sequence of three opinions—Hirabayashi, Korematsu, and Endo. There was no reason to think that Gordon Hirabayashi and Fred Korematsu were any less loyal to the United States than was Mitsuye Endo. Presumably they would have been entitled to relief from detention upon the same showing as that made by Endo. But even had Hirabayashi tried to raise that question in his case, he would have failed, for the Court chose to confine itself to the curfew issue. It was not until we were clearly winning the war that the Court came around to this view in Endo. The process illustrates in a rough way the Latin maxim Inter arma silent leges (in time of war the laws are silent).

Postwar public opinion very quickly came to see the forced relocation and detention of people of Japanese ancestry as a grave injustice. Writing in 1945, Eugene Rostow, then a professor at Yale Law School and later its dean, declared the program "a disaster" that both represented an abandonment of our traditional subordination of military to civil authority and sanctioned racially based discrimination. Edward Ennis, who as a lawyer in the Justice Department had opposed the program, reappeared nearly forty years later on behalf of the ACLU to testify before the congressionally created Commission on Wartime Relocation and Internment of Civilians. He characterized the program as "the worst blow to civil liberty in our history." In the view of this author, some of this criticism is well justified, and some not; its principal fault is that it lumps together the cases of the issei and the nisei.

The cases before the Supreme Court—Hirabayashi, Korematsu, and Endo—all involved nisei, children of immigrants, who were born in the United States and thus were American. The basis on which the Court upheld the plan were military representations as to the necessity for evacuation. These representations were undoubtedly exaggerated, and they were based in part on the view that not only the issei but their children were different from other West Coast residents.

In defense of the military it should be pointed out that these officials were not entrusted with the protection of anyone's civil liberty; their job was making sure that vital areas were as secure as possible from espionage or sabotage. The role of General DeWitt was not one to encourage a nice calculation of the costs in civil liberty as opposed to the benefits to national security. Gen. Walter Short, the Army commander in Hawaii, and Adm. Husband E. Kimmel, the Navy commander there, both were summarily removed from their commands ten days after Pearl Harbor because of their failure to anticipate the Japanese surprise attack. The head of the Western Defense command was surely going to err on the side of preparedness.

Moreover, it was not DeWitt and his associates who had first recommended evacuation of the issei and nisei; as we have seen, the principal early proponents of that idea were Governor Olson, Attorney General Warren, Los Angeles Mayor Bowron, and the congressional delegations of the three West Coast states. Public opinion should not be the determining factor in making a military appraisal, but it is bound to occur to those engaged in that task how they will be regarded if they reject a widely popular security measure that in retrospect turns out to have been necessary.

The United States prides itself on having a system in which the civilian heads of the service departments are supreme over the military chiefs, so one might expect that Henry Stimson and John McCloy would have made a more careful evaluation of the evacuation proposal than they appear to have done. Far from the Pacific Coast, they would be expected to have a more detached view than the commander on the scene. But here too there seems to have been a tendency to feel that concern for civil liberty was not their responsibility. There is even more of this feeling in Roosevelt's perfunctory approval of the plan in response to a phone call from Stimson. Biddle's protests proved futile even at the highest levels of government, in part because no significant element of public opinion opposed the relocation.

Once the relocation plan was in place, it could be challenged only in the courts. Was the Supreme Court at fault in upholding first the curfew, in Hirabayashi, and then the relocation, in Korematsu? In Hirabayashi the Court could have decided both the validity of the relocation requirement and the curfew requirement, for the "concurrent sentence" doctrine under which it declined to do so is discretionary. But counseling against any broader decision was the well-established rule that the Court should avoid deciding constitutional questions if at all possible, and so the Hirabayashi decision left the far more difficult question for another day.

When that day came, in Korematsu, a majority of the Court upheld the relocation program. Justice Black's opinion for the Court in Korematsu followed the same line of reasoning as had Chief Justice Stone's in Hirabayashi. But this time there were three dissenters, who had voted to uphold the curfew but wanted to strike down the relocation program.

Over the years, several criticisms have been made of the Court's opinions in these cases. The most general is of its extremely deferential treatment given to the government's argument that the curfew and relocation were necessitated by military considerations. Here one can only echo Justice Jackson's observation that "in the very nature of things, military decisions are not susceptible of intelligent judicial appraisal." But it surely does not follow from this that a court must therefore invalidate measures based on military judgments. Eugene Rostow suggested holding a judicial inquiry into the entire question of military necessity, but this seems an extraordinarily dubious proposition. Judicial inquiry, with its restrictive rules of evidence, orientation toward resolution of factual disputes in individual cases, and long delays, is ill suited to determine an urgent issue. The necessity for prompt action was cogently stated by the Court in its Hirabayashi opinion: "Although the results of the attack on Pearl Harbor were not fully disclosed until much later, it was known that the damage was extensive, and that the Japanese by their successes had gained a naval superiority over our forces in the Pacific which might enable them to seize Pearl Harbor, our largest naval base and the last stronghold of defense lying between Japan and the west coast. That reasonably prudent men charged with the responsibility of our national defense had ample ground for concluding that they must face the danger of invasion, take measures against it, and in making the choice of measures consider our internal situation, cannot be doubted."

The second criticism is that the decisions in these cases upheld a program that, at bottom, was based on racial distinctions. There are several levels at which this criticism can be made. The broadest is that the nisei were relocated simply because the Caucasian majority on the West Coast (and in the country as a whole) disliked them and wished to remove them as neighbors or as business competitors. The Court's answer to this attack seems satisfactory: Those of Japanese descent were displaced because of fear that disloyal elements among them would aid Japan in the war. Though there were undoubtedly nativists in California who welcomed a chance to see the issei and the nisei removed, it does not follow that this point of view was attributable to the military decisionmakers. They, after all, did not at first propose relocation. But a narrower criticism along the same line has more force to it: The nisei were evacuated notwithstanding the fact that they were American citizens. Even in wartime citizens may not be rounded up and required to prove their loyalty. They may be excluded from sensitive military areas in the absence of a security clearance and otherwise be denied access to any classified information, but it pushes these propositions to an extreme to say that a sizable geographic area, including the homes of many citizens, may be declared off-limits and the residents forced to move. It pushes it to an even greater extreme to say that such persons may be required not only to leave their homes but to report to and remain in a distant relocation center.

The Supreme Court in its Hirabayashi opinion pointed to several facts thought to justify this treatment of the nisei. Both federal and state restrictions on the rights of Japanese emigrants had prevented their assimilation into the Caucasian population and had intensified their insularity and solidarity. Japanese parents sent their children to Japanese-language schools, and there was some evidence that these were a source of Japanese nationalistic propaganda. As many as ten thousand American-born children of Japanese parentage went to Japan for all or a part of their education. Thus, as Stone put it in his opinion, "we cannot say that the war-making branches of the Government did not have ground for believing that in a critical hour such persons . . . constituted a menace to the national defense and safety. . ." There is considerable irony, of course, in relying on previously existing laws discriminating against Japanese immigrants to conclude that still further disabilities should be imposed upon them because they had not been assimilated into the Caucasian majority. But in time of war a nation may be required to respond to a condition without making a careful inquiry into how that condition came about.

Were the condition or conditions described by the Court sufficient to justify treating the nisei differently from all other citizens on the West Coast? Under today's constitutional law, certainly not. Any sort of "racial" classification by government is viewed as suspect, and an extraordinarily strong reason is required to justify it.

But the law was by no means so clear when these cases were decided. A decade later the Court decided the watershed case of Brown v. Board of Education, holding that the Kansas legislature had violated the Equal Protection Clause of the Fourteenth Amendment by permitting public schools to segregate students by race. And with Brown there was argued a companion case, Bolling v. Sharpe, challenging similarly imposed segregation in public schools in the District of Columbia. This requirement had been imposed not by a state government but by Congress. The Court in Bolling, in a brief opinion not notable for clarity of reasoning, held that the Due Process Clause of the Fifth Amendment imposes on the federal government a limitation similar to that imposed on the states by the Equal Protection Clause of the Fourteenth Amendment. Had this doctrine been the law ten years earlier, the Supreme Court might have found it easier to reach a different result in Hirabayashi and Korematsu.

The discrimination against the nisei lay in the fact that any other citizen could remain in his home unless actually tried and convicted of espionage or sabotage while the nisei were removed from their homes without any individualized findings at all. The proffered justification—that an attack on the West Coast by Japan was reasonably feared and that American citizens of Japanese descent were more likely than the populace as a whole to include potential spies or saboteurs—was not wholly groundless. A May 1941 "Magic intercept," resulting from the Americans' having broken the Japanese code, contained a message from the Japanese consulate in Los Angeles that "we also have connections with our second generations working in airplane plants for intelligence purposes." But although such information might well have justified exclusion of nisei, as opposed to other citizens, from work in aircraft factories without strict security clearance, it falls considerably short of justifying the dislodging of thousands of citizens from their homes on the basis of ancestry.

The issei, however, who were not citizens, were both by tradition and by law in a quite different category. The legal difference dates back to the Alien Enemies Law enacted in 1798 during the administration of President John Adams. The Alien Law is often bracketed together with the Sedition Act passed at the same time, and there is a tendency to think that both were repealed as soon as Thomas Jefferson and his Jeffersonian Republicans came to power in 1801. But only the Sedition Act was repealed; the Alien Enemies Act, with minor amendments, remained on the books at the time of World War II. It provided: "Whenever there shall be a declared war between the United States and any foreign nation or government . . . all natives, citizens, denizens, or subjects of the hostile nation or government, being of the age of fourteen years and upward, who shall be within the United States and not actually naturalized, shall be liable to be apprehended, restrained, secured, and removed as alien enemies."

In a case decided shortly after the end of World War II, the Supreme Court, referring to the Alien Law, said: "Executive power over enemy aliens, undelayed and unhampered by litigation, has been deemed, throughout our history, essential to war-time security. This is in keeping with the practice of the most enlightened of nations and has resulted in treatment of alien enemies more considerate than that which has prevailed among any of our enemies and some of our allies. This statute was enacted or suffered to continue by men who helped found the Republic and formulate the Bill of Rights, and although it obviously denies enemy aliens the constitutional immunities of citizens, it seems not then to have been supposed that a nation's obligations to its foes could ever be put on a parity with those to its defenders. The resident enemy alien is constitutionally subject to summary arrest, internment and deportation whenever a 'declared war' exists." Thus distinctions that might not be permissible between classes of citizens must be viewed otherwise when drawn between classes of aliens. The most frequently made charge on behalf of the issei is that the government treated Japanese enemy aliens differently from enemy aliens of German or Italian citizenship when we were at war with all three countries. It appears that there was some removal of Italian enemy aliens for a brief period, but there seems little doubt that the West Coast issei were treated differently from the majority of German or Italian nationals residing in this country. It should be pointed out, however, that there does not appear to have been the same concentration of German or Italian nationals along the West Coast in areas near major defense plants. Japanese emigration to the United States had occurred only within the preceding half-century, and the emigrants resided almost entirely on the West Coast, where U.S. aircraft production was highly concentrated and where attack and possibly invasion were at first feared. Italian emigration had taken place over a considerably longer period, and German since colonial days, and people of German and Italian ancestry were far more spread out in the population in general than were the issei.

These distinctions seem insufficient to justify such a sharp difference of treatment between Japanese and German and Italian aliens in peacetime. But they do seem legally adequate to support the difference in treatment between the two classes of enemy aliens in time of war.

An entirely separate and important philosophical question is whether occasional presidential excesses and judicial restraint in wartime are desirable or undesirable. In one sense this question is very largely academic. There is no reason to think that future wartime Presidents will act differently from Roosevelt or that future Justices of the Supreme Court will decide questions differently from their predecessors. But even though this be so, there is every reason to believe that the historic trend against the least justified of the curtailments of civil liberty in wartime will continue in the future. It is neither desirable nor remotely likely that civil liberty will occupy as favored a position in wartime as it does in peacetime.

But it is both desirable and likely that the courts will pay more careful attention to the basis for the government's claims of necessity as a reason for curtailing civil liberty. The laws will thus not be silent in time of war, even though they will speak with a somewhat different voice.

October 1998

Questions:

(1.) On the basis of what you have read, do you believe that President Franklin Roosevelt and the government had legitimate enough concerns about national security to single out Japanese-Americans for confinement for the duration of the Second World War? Or, do you believe that the policy was the result of nationalism and/or racial prejudice?

(2.) The law makes a distinction between classes of citizens and classes of alien residents. Do you think it makes sense to allow the government to treat the latter – who are, after all, residing legally in the United States – more harshly in time of war?

(3.) Could something like the internment of Japanese-Americans happen again? Can you imagine a set of circumstances today in which an American president would try to place a certain ethnic group of American citizens into confinement – and have the popular support of the American people in doing so? If so, should the courts be more assertive than previously in examining the government's rationale for curtailing civil liberties?

112

CHAPTER 11

THE TRIUMPH OF WATERGATE

Walter Karp and Vance Bourjaily

Walter Karp offers interesting insights in his look back at Watergate. Reading "The Triumph of Watergate," we consider again the breech of public confidence that Watergate represented. Karp describes the extent of the Watergate coverup and chastises the Congress for not acting sooner. While the "Lessons of Watergate" are often mentioned, it is worth reflecting on what the American public actually learned. Some argue that the lasting legacy of Watergate is a cynism and distrust toward politicians that has weakened government. Can government operate in a climate of skepticism? What factors restore and build public trust?

Ten years after Richard M. Nixon was forced to resign his office rather than submit to impeachment, two authors reconsidered the events of that incredible summer.

I. THE HOUR OF THE FOUNDERS
WALTER KARP

Exactly ten years ago this August, the thirty-seventh President of the United States, facing imminent impeachment, resigned his high office and passed out of our lives. "The system worked," the nation exclaimed, heaving a sigh of relief. What had brought that relief was the happy extinction of the prolonged fear that the "system" might not work at all. But what was it that had inspired such fears? When I asked myself that question recently, I found I could scarcely, remember. Although I had followed the Watergate crisis with minute attention, it had grown vague and formless in my mind, like a nightmare recollected in sunshine. It was not until I began working my way through back copies of the *New York Times* that I was able to remember clearly why I used to read my morning paper with forebodings for the country's future.

The Watergate crisis had begun in June 1972 as a "third-rate burglary" of the Democratic National Committee headquarters in Washington's Watergate building complex. By late March 1973 the burglary and subsequent efforts to obstruct its investigation had been laid at the door of the White House. By late June, Americans were asking themselves whether their President had or had

not ordered the payment of "hush money" to silence a Watergate burglar. Investi-
gated by a special Senate committee headed by Sam Ervin of North Carolina, the scandal continued to deepen and ramify during the summer of 1973. By March 1974 the third-rate burglary of 1972 had grown into an unprecedented constitutional crisis.

By then it was clear beyond doubt that President Richard M. Nixon stood at the center of a junto of henchmen without parallel in our history. One of Nixon's attorneys general, John Mitchell, was indicted for obstructing justice in Washington and for impeding a Securities and Exchange Commission investigation in New York. Another, Richard Kleindienst, had criminally misled the Senate Judiciary Committee in the President's interest. The acting director of the Federal Bureau of Investigation, L. Patrick Gray, had burned incriminating White House documents at the behest of a presidential aide. Bob Haldeman, the President's chief of staff, John Ehrlichman, the President's chief domestic adviser, and Charles Colson, the President's special counsel, all had been indicted for obstructing justice in the investigation of the Watergate burglary. John Dean, the President's legal counsel and chief accuser, had already pleaded guilty to the same charge. Dwight Chapin, the President's appointments secretary, faced trial for lying to a grand jury about political sabotage carried out during the 1972 elections. Ehrlichman and two other White House aides were under indictment for conspiring to break into a psychiatrist's office and steal confidential information about one of his former patients, Daniel Ellsberg. By March 1974 some twenty-eight presidential aides or election officials had been indicted for crimes carried out in the President's interest. Never before in American history had a President so signally failed to fulfill his constitutional duty to "take care that the laws be faithfully executed."

It also had been clear for many months that the thirty-seventh President of the United States did not feel bound by his constitutional duties. He insisted that the requirements of national security as he and he alone saw fit to define it, released him from the most fundamental legal and constitutional constraints. In the name of "national security," the President had created a secret band of private detectives, paid with private funds, to carry out political espionage at the urging of the White House. In the name of "national security," the President had approved the warrantless wiretapping of news reporters. In the name of "national security," he had approved a secret plan for massive, illegal surveillance of American citizens. He had encouraged his aides' efforts to use the Internal Revenue Service to harass political "enemies"—prominent Americans who endangered "national security" by publicly criticizing the President's Vietnam War policies.

The framers of the Constitution had provided one and only one remedy for such lawless abuse of power: impeachment in the House of Representatives and trial in the Senate for "high Crimes and Misdemeanors." There was absolutely no alternative. If Congress had not held President Nixon accountable for lawless conduct of his office, then Congress would have condoned a lawless Presidency. If Congress had not struck from the President's hands the despot's cudgel of "national security," then Congress would have condoned a despotic Presidency.

Looking through the back issues of the *New York Times*, I recollected in a flood of ten-year-old memories what it was that had filled me with such foreboding. It was the reluctance of Congress to act. I felt anew my fury when members of Congress pretended that nobody really cared about Watergate except the "media" and the "Nixon-haters." The real folks "back home," they said, cared only about inflation and the gasoline shortage. I remembered the exasperating actions of leading Democrats, such as a certain Senate leader who went around telling the country that President Nixon could not be impeached because in America a person was presumed innocent until proven guilty. Surely the senator knew that impeachment was not a verdict of guilt but a formal accusation made in the House leading to trial in the Senate. Why was he muddying the waters, I wondered, if not to protect the President? It had taken one of the most outrageous episodes in the history of the Presidency to compel Congress to make even a pretense of action.

Back on July 16, 1973, a former White House aide named Alexander Butterfield had told the Ervin committee that President Nixon secretly tape-recorded his most intimate political conversations. On two solemn occasions that spring the President had sworn to the American people that he knew nothing of the Watergate cover-up until his counsel John Dean had told him about it on March 21, 1973. From that day forward, Nixon had said, "I began intensive new inquiries into this whole matter." Now we learned that the President had kept evidence secret that would exonerate him completely—if he were telling the truth. Worse yet, he wanted it kept secret. Before Butterfield had revealed the existence of the tapes, the President had grandly announced that "executive privilege will not be invoked as to any testimony [by my aides] concerning possible criminal conduct, in the matters under investigation. I want the public to learn the truth about Watergate. . . . " After the existence of the tapes was revealed, however, the President showed the most ferocious resistance to disclosing the "truth about Watergate." He now claimed that executive privilege—hitherto a somewhat shadowy presidential prerogative— gave a President "absolute power" to withhold any taped conversation he chose, even those urgently needed in the ongoing criminal investigation then being conducted by a special Watergate prosecutor. Nixon even claimed, through his lawyers, that the judicial branch of the federal government was "absolutely without power to reweigh that choice or to make a different resolution of it."

In the U.S. Court of Appeals the special prosecutor, a Harvard Law School professor named Archibald Cox, called the President's claim "intolerable."

Millions of Americans found it infuriating. The court found it groundless. On October 12, 1973, it ordered the President to surrender nine taped conversations that Cox had been fighting to obtain for nearly three months.

Determined to evade the court order, the President on October 19 announced that he had devised a "compromise." Instead of handing over the recorded conversations to the court, he would submit only edited summaries. To verify their truthfulness, the President would allow Sen. John Stennis of Mississippi to listen to the tapes. As an independent verifier, the elderly senator was distinguished by his devotion to the President's own overblown conception of a "strong" Presidency. When Nixon had ordered the secret bombing of Cambodia, he had vouch-safed the fact to Senator Stennis, who thought that concealing the President's secret war from his fellow senators was a higher duty than preserving the Senate's constitutional role in the formation of United States foreign policy.

On Saturday afternoon, October 20, I and millions of other Americans sat by our television sets while the special prosecutor explained why he could not accept "what seems to me to be non-compliance with the court's order." Then the President flashed the dagger sheathed within his "compromise." At 8:31 P.M. television viewers across the country learned that he had fired the special prosecutor; that attorney general Elliot Richardson had resigned rather than issue that order to Cox; that the deputy attorney general, William Ruckelshaus, also had refused to do so and had been fired for refusing; that it was a third acting attorney general who had finally issued the order. With trembling voices, television newscasters reported that the President had abolished the office of special prosecutor and that the FBI was standing guard over its files. Never before in our history had a President, setting law at defiance, made our government seem so tawdry and gimcrack. "It's like living in a banana republic," a friend of mine remarked.

Now the question before the country was clear. "Whether ours shall continue to be a government of laws and not of men," the ex-special prosecutor said that evening, "is now for the Congress and ultimately the American people to decide."

Within ten days of the "Saturday night massacre," one million letters and telegrams rained down on Congress, almost every one of them demanding the President's impeachment. But congressional leaders dragged their feet. The House Judiciary Committee would begin an inquiry into *whether* to begin an inquiry into possible grounds for recommending impeachment to the House. With the obvious intent, it seemed to me, of waiting until the impeachment fervor had abated, the Democratic-controlled committee would consider whether to consider making a recommendation about making an accusation.

Republicans hoped to avoid upholding the rule of law by persuading the President to resign. This attempt to supply a lawless remedy for lawless power earned Republicans a memorable rebuke from one of the most venerated members of their party: eighty-one-year-old Sen. George Aiken of Vermont. The demand for Nixon's resignation, he said, "suggests that many prominent Americans, who ought to know better, find the task of holding a President accountable as just too difficult. . . . To ask the President now to resign and thus relieve Congress of its clear congressional duty amounts to a declaration of incompetence on the part of Congress."

The system was manifestly not working. But neither was the President's defense. On national television Nixon bitterly assailed the press for its "outrageous, vicious, distorted" reporting, but the popular outrage convinced him, nonetheless, to surrender the nine tapes to the court. Almost at once the White House tapes began their singular career of encompassing the President's ruin. On October 31 the White House disclosed that two of the taped conversations were missing, including one between the President and his campaign manager, John Mitchell, which had taken place the day after Nixon returned from a Florida vacation and three days after the Watergate break-in. Three weeks later the tapes dealt Nixon a more potent blow. There was an eighteen-and-a-half-minute gap, the White House announced, in a taped conversation between the President and Haldeman, which had also taken place the day after he returned from Florida. The White House suggested first that the President's secretary, Rose Mary Woods, had accidentally erased part of the tape while transcribing it. When the loyal Miss Woods could not demonstrate in court how she could have pressed the "erase" button unwittingly for eighteen straight minutes, the White House attributed the gap to "some sinister force." On January 15, 1974, court-appointed experts provided a more humdrum explanation. The gap had been produced by at least five manual erasures. Someone in the White House had deliberately destroyed evidence that might have proved that President Nixon knew of the Watergate cover-up from the start.

At this point the Judiciary Committee was in its third month of considering whether to consider. But by now there was scarcely an American who did not think the President guilty, and on February 6, 1974, the House voted 410 to 4 to authorize the Judiciary Committee to begin investigating possible grounds for impeaching the President of the United States. It had taken ten consecutive months of the most damning revelations of criminal misconduct, a titanic outburst of public indignation, and an unbroken record of presidential deceit, defiance, and evasion in order to compel Congress to take its first real step. That long record of immobility and feigned indifference boded ill for the future.

The White House knew how to exploit congressional reluctance. One tactic involved a highly technical but momentous question: What constituted an impeachable offense? On February 21 the staff of the Judiciary Committee had issued a report. Led by two distinguished attorneys, John Doar, a fifty-two-year- old Wisconsin Independent, and Albert Jenner, a sixty-seven-year-old Chicago Republican, the staff had taken the broad view of impeachment for which Hamilton and Madison had contended in *The Federalist Papers*. Despite the constitutional phrase "high Crimes and Misdemeanors," the staff report had argued that an impeachable offense did not have to be a crime. "Some of the most grievous offenses against our Constitutional form of government may not entail violations of the criminal law."

The White House launched a powerful counterattack. At a news conference on February 25, the President contended that only proven criminal misconduct supplied grounds for impeachment. On February 28, the White House drove home his point with a tightly argued legal paper: If a President could be impeached for anything other than a crime of "a very serious nature," it would expose the Presidency to "political impeachments."

The argument was plausible. But if Congress accepted it, the Watergate crisis could only end in disaster. Men of great power do not commit crimes. They procure crimes without having to issue incriminating orders. A word to the servile suffices. "Who will free me from this turbulent priest," asked Henry II, and four of his barons bashed in the skull of Thomas à Becket. The ease with which the powerful can arrange "deniability," to use the Watergate catchword, was one reason the criminal standard was so dangerous to liberty. Instead of having to take care that the laws be faithfully executed, a President, under that standard, would only have to take care to insulate himself from the criminal activities of his agents. Moreover, the standard could not reach the most dangerous offenses. There is no crime in the statute books called "attempted tyranny."

Yet the White House campaign to narrow the definition of impeachment met with immediate success. In March one of the members of the House of Representatives said that before voting to impeach Nixon, he would "want to know beyond a reasonable doubt that he was directly involved in the commission of a crime." To impeach the President for the grave abuse of his powers, lawmakers said, would be politically impossible. On the Judiciary Committee itself the senior Republican, Edward Hutchinson of Michigan, disavowed the staff's view of impeachment and adopted the President's. Until the final days of the crisis, the criminal definition of impeachment was to hang over the country's fate like the sword of Damocles.

The criminal standard buttressed the President's larger thesis: In defending himself he was fighting to protect the "Presidency" from sinister forces trying to "weaken" it. On March 12 the President's lawyer, James D. St. Clair, sounded this theme when he declared that he did not represent the President "individually" but rather the "office of the Presidency." There was even a National Citizens Committee for Fairness to the Presidency. It was America's global leadership, Nixon insisted, that made a "strong" Presidency so essential. Regardless of the opinion of some members of the Judiciary Committee, Nixon told a joint session of Congress, he would do nothing that "impairs the ability of the Presidents of the future to make the great decisions that are so essential to this nation and the world."

I used to listen to statements such as these with deep exasperation. Here was a President daring to tell Congress, in effect, that a lawless Presidency was necessary to America's safety, while a congressional attempt to reassert the rule of law undermined the nation's security.

Fortunately for constitutional government, however, Nixon's conception of a strong Presidency included one prerogative whose exercise was in itself an impeachable offense. Throughout the month of March the President insisted that the need for "confidentiality" allowed him to withhold forty-two tapes that the Judiciary Committee had asked of him. Nixon was claiming the right to limit the constitutional power of Congress to inquire into his impeachment. This was more than Republicans on the committee could afford to tolerate.

"Ambition must be made to counteract ambition, "Madison had written in *The Federalist*. On April 11 the Judiciary Committee voted 33 to 3 to subpoena the forty-two tapes, the first subpoena ever issued to a President by a committee of the House. Ambition, at last, was counteracting ambition. This set the stage for one of the most lurid moments in the entire Watergate crisis.

As the deadline for compliance drew near, tension began mounting in the country. Comply or defy? Which would the President do? Open defiance was plainly impeachable. Frank compliance was presumably ruinous. On Monday, April 29, the President went on television to give the American people his answer. Seated in the Oval Office with the American flag behind him, President Nixon calmly announced that he was going to make over to the Judiciary Committee—and the public—"edited transcripts" of the subpoenaed tapes. These transcripts "Will tell it all," said the President; there was nothing more that would need to be known for an impeachment inquiry about his conduct. To sharpen the public impression of presidential candor, the transcripts had been distributed among forty-two thick, loose-leaf binders, which were stacked in two-foot-high piles by the President's desk. As if to warn the public not to trust what the newspapers would say about the transcripts, Nixon accused the media of concocting the Watergate crisis out of "rumor, gossip, innuendo," of creating a "vague, general impression of massive wrongdoing, implicating everybody, gaining credibility by its endless repetition."

The next day's *New York Times* pronounced the President's speech "his most powerful Watergate defense since the scandal broke." By May 1 James Reston, the newspaper's most eminent columnist, thought the President had "probably gained considerable support in the country." For a few days it seemed as though the President had pulled off a coup. Republicans on the Judiciary Committee acted accordingly. On the first of May, 16 of the 17 committee Republicans voted against sending the President a note advising him that self-edited transcripts punctured by hundreds upon hundreds of suspicious "inaudibles" and "unintelligibles" were not in compliance with the committee's subpoena. The President, it was said, had succeeded in making impeachment look "partisan" and consequently discreditable.

Not even bowdlerized transcripts, however, could nullify the destructive power of those tapes. They revealed a White House steeped in more sordid conniving than Nixon's worst enemies had imagined. They showed a President advising his aides on how to "stonewall" a grand jury without committing perjury: "You can say, 'I don't remember.' You can say, 'I can't recall. I can't give any answer to that, that I can recall.'" They showed a President urging his counsel to make a "complete report" about Watergate but to "make it very incomplete." They showed a President eager for vengeance against ordinary election opponents. "I want the most comprehensive notes on all those who tried to do us in. . . . They are asking for it and they are going to get it." It showed a President discussing how "national security grounds" might be invoked to justify the Ellsberg burglary should the secret ever come out. "I think we could get by on that," replies Nixon's counsel.

On May 7 Pennsylvania's Hugh Scott, Senate Republican Minority Leader, pronounced the revelations in the transcript "disgusting, shabby, immoral performances." Joseph Alsop, who had long been friendly toward the President in his column, compared the atmosphere in the Oval Office to the "back room of a second-rate advertising agency in a suburb of hell." A week after Nixon's seeming coup Republicans were once again vainly urging him to resign. On May 9 the House Judiciary Committee staff began presenting to the members its massive accumulation of Watergate material. Since the presentation was made behind closed doors, a suspenseful lull fell over the Watergate battleground.

Over the next two months it was obvious that the Judiciary Committee was growing increasingly impatient with the President, who continued to insist that, even in an impeachment proceeding, the "executive must remain the final arbiter of demands on its confidentiality." When Nixon refused to comply in any way with a second committee subpoena, the members voted 28 to 10 to warn him that "your refusals in and of themselves might constitute a ground for impeach- ment." The "partisanship" of May 1 had faded by May 30.

Undermining these signs of decisiveness was the continued insistence that only direct presidential involvement in a crime would be regarded as an impeachable offense in the House. Congressmen demanded to see the "smoking gun." They wanted to be shown the "hand in the cookie jar." Alexander Hamilton had called impeachment a "National Inquest." Congress seemed bent on restricting it to the purview of a local courthouse. Nobody spoke of the larger issues. As James Reston noted on May 26, one of the most disturbing aspects of Watergate was the silence of the prominent. Where, Reston asked, were the educators, the business leaders, and the elder statesmen to delineate and define the great constitutional issues at stake? When the White House began denouncing the Judiciary Committee as a "lynch mob," virtually nobody rose to the committee's defense.

On July 7 the Sunday edition of the *New York Times* made doleful reading. "The official investigations seem beset by semitropical torpor," the newspaper reported in its weekly news summary. White House attacks on the committee, said the *Times*, were proving effective in the country. In March, 60 percent of those polled by Gallup wanted the President tried in the Senate for his misdeeds. By June the figure had fallen to 50 percent. The movement for impeachment, said the *Times*, was losing its momentum. Nixon, it seemed, had worn out the public capacity for righteous indignation.

Then, on July 19, John Doar, the Democrats' counsel, did what nobody had done before with the enormous, confusing mass of interconnected misdeeds that we labeled "Watergate" for sheer convenience. At a meeting of the Judiciary Committee he compressed the endlessly ramified scandal into a grave and compelling case for impeaching the thirty-seventh President of the United States. He spoke of the President's "enormous crimes." He warned the committee that it dare not look indifferently upon the "terrible deed of subverting the Constitution." He urged the members to consider with favor five broad articles of impeachment, charges with a grave historic ring, as the *Times* said of them.

In a brief statement, Albert Jenner, the Republicans' counsel, strongly endorsed Doar's recommendations. The Founding Fathers, he reminded committee members, had established a free country and a free Constitution. It was now the committee's momentous duty to determine "whether that country and that Constitution are to be preserved."

How I had yearned for those words during the long, arid months of the "smoking gun" and the "hand in the cookie jar." Members of the committee must have felt the same way, too, for Jenner's words were to leave a profound mark on their final deliberations. That I did not know yet, but what I did know was heartening. The grave maxims of liberty, once invoked, instantly took the measure of meanness and effrontery. When the President's press spokesman, Ron Ziegler, denounced the committee's proceedings as a "kangaroo court," a wave of disgust coursed through Congress. The hour of the Founders had arrived. The final deliberations of the House Judiciary Committee began on the evening of July 24, when Chairman Peter Rodino gaveled the committee to order before some forty-five million television viewers. The committee made a curious spectacle: thirty-eight strangers strung out on a two-tiered dais, a huge piece of furniture as unfamiliar as the faces of its occupants.

Chairman Rodino made the first opening remarks. His public career had been long, unblemished, and thoroughly undistinguished. Now the representative from Newark, New Jersey, linked hands with the Founding Fathers of our government. "For more than two years, there have been serious allegations, by people of good faith and sound intelligence, that the President, Richard M. Nixon, has committed grave and systematic violations of the Constitution."

The framers of our Constitution, said Rodino, had provided an exact measure of a President's responsibilities. It was by the terms of the President's oath of office, prescribed in the Constitution, that the framers intended to hold Presidents "accountable and lawful."

That was to prove the keynote. That evening and over the following days, as each committee member delivered a statement, it became increasingly clear that the broad maxims of constitutional supremacy had taken command of the impeachment inquiry. "We will by this impeachment proceeding be establishing a standard of conduct for the President of the United States which will for all time be a matter of public record," Caldwell Butler, a conservative Virginia Republican, reminded his conservative constituents. "If we fail to impeach . . . we will have left condoned and unpunished an abuse of power totally without justification."

There were still White House loyalists of course; men who kept demanding to see a presidential directive ordering a crime and a documented "tie-in" between Nixon and his henchmen. Set against the great principle of constitutional supremacy, however, this common view was now exposed for what it was: reckless trifling with our ancient liberties. Can the United States permit a President "to escape accountability because he may choose to deal behind closed doors," asked James Mann, a South Carolina conservative. "Can anyone argue," asked George Danielson, a California liberal, "that if a President breaches his oath of office, he should not be removed?" In a voice of unforgettable power and richness, Barbara Jordan, a black legislator from Texas, sounded the grand theme of the committee with particular depth of feeling. Once, she said, the Constitution had excluded people of her race, but that evil had been remedied. "My faith in the Constitution is whole, it is complete, it is total and I am not going to sit here and be an idle spectator to the diminution, the subversion, the destruction of the Constitution."

On July 27 the Judiciary Committee voted 27 to 11 (six Republicans joining all twenty-one Democrats) to impeach Richard Nixon on the grounds that he and his agents had "prevented, obstructed, and impeded the administration of justice" in "violation of his constitutional oath faithfully to execute the office of President of the United States and, to the best of his ability, preserve, protect, and defend the Constitution of the United States, and in violation of his constitutional duty to take care that the laws be faithfully executed."

On July 29 the Judiciary Committee voted 28 to 10 to impeach Richard Nixon for "violating the constitutional rights of citizens, impairing the due and proper administration of justice and the conduct of lawful inquiries, or contravening the laws governing agencies of the executive branch. . . . " Thus, the illegal wiretaps, the sinister White House spies, the attempted use of the IRS to punish political opponents, the abuse of the CIA, and the break-in at Ellsberg's psychiatrist's office—misconduct hitherto deemed too "vague" for impeachment—now became part of a President's impeachable failure to abide by his constitutional oath to carry out his constitutional duty.

Lastly, on July 30 the Judiciary Committee, hoping to protect some future impeachment inquiry from a repetition of Nixon's defiance, voted 21 to 17 to impeach him for refusing to comply with the committee's subpoenas. "This concludes the work of the committee," Rodino announced at eleven o'clock that night. Armed with the wisdom of the Founders and the authority of America's republican principles, the committee had cut through the smoke screens, the lies, and the pettifogging that had muddled the Watergate crisis for so many months. It had subjected an imperious Presidency to the rule of fundamental law. It had demonstrated by resounding majorities that holding a President accountable is neither "liberal" nor "conservative," neither "Democratic" nor "Republican," but something far more basic to the American republic.

For months the forces of evasion had claimed that impeachment would "tear the country apart." But now the country was more united than it had been in years. The impeachment inquiry had sounded the chords of deepest patriotism, and Americans responded, it seemed to me, with quiet pride in their country and themselves. On Capitol Hill, congressional leaders reported that Nixon's impeachment would command three hundred votes at a minimum. The Senate began preparing for the President's trial. Then, as countless wits remarked, a funny thing happened on the way to the forum.

Back on July 24, the day the Judiciary Committee began its televised deliberations, the Supreme Court had ordered the President to surrender sixty-four taped conversations subpoenaed by the Watergate prosecutor. At the time I had regarded the decision chiefly as an auspicious omen for the evening's proceedings. Only Richard Nixon knew that the Court had signed his death warrant. On August 5 the President announced that he was making public three tapes that "may further damage my case." In fact they destroyed what little was left of it. Recorded six days after the Watergate break-in, they showed the President discussing detailed preparations for the cover-up with his chief of staff, Bob Haldeman. They showed the President and his henchman discussing how to use the CIA to block the FBI, which was coming dangerously close to the White House. "You call them in," says the President. "Good deal," says his aide. In short, the three tapes proved that the President had told nothing but lies about Watergate for twenty-six months. Every one of Nixon's ten Judiciary Committee defenders now announced that he favored Nixon's impeachment.

The President still had one last evasion: on the evening of August 8 he appeared on television to make his last important announcement. "I no longer have a strong enough political base in Congress," said Nixon, doing his best to imply that the resolution of a great constitutional crisis was mere maneuvering for political advantage. "Therefore, I shall resign the Presidency effective at noon tomorrow." He admitted to no wrongdoing. If he had made mistakes of judgment, "they were made in what I believed at the time to be in the best interests of the nation."

On the morning of August 9 the first President ever to resign from office boarded Air Force One and left town. The "system" had worked. But in the watches of the night, who has not asked himself now and then: How would it all have turned out had there been no White House tapes?

II. THE FINAL ACT
VANCE BOURJAILY

At the time of Richard Nixon's resignation from the Presidency, columnists, politicians, and other sages spoke woefully of the tragedy of Watergate, or the trauma of Watergate, depending on whether their sense of language was Shakespearean or psychiatric. They were, in either case, Washington folk, and apparently not much aware that many of us, out in the country, looked on the thing more as the triumph of Watergate, or even, depending on the length of our standing as Nixon-haters, the Watergate comedy hour—with Groucho Liddy, Harpo Hunt in the red wig, and the President as Zeppo, the straight brother who sings at the end of the show. Martha Mitchell was perfect as Margaret Dumont, and there were several candidates for Chico, Charles Colson for one, though my favorite was Donald Segretti, the busy young California lawyer who signed himself on as an expert in dirty tricks.

If there were gleeful, hard-nosed scapegraces who watched Watergate that way, our laughter had, I confess, a paranoid nervousness much of the time. We could never feel sure that Nixon, Haig, and Kissinger would not engineer America's first military take-over, in preference to its first presidential act of self- destruction. Not until we saw the final helicopter lift off from the White House garden could we really relax and enjoy it all.

I enjoy it less in perspective, and I sympathize more with the leading player. I have come to see Watergate not as a complete tragedy but as the last act of a terribly extended one, which opened in crazy violence with the assassination of John Kennedy.

It was Greek in form, rather than Elizabethan, a democratic rather than a royal tragedy. This was largely because of the participation of a chorus of around two hundred million. Much of the long sequence concerned the fall of the great Kennedy family, whose antagonist Nixon was. But interwoven was the division of a once-united nation, whose people passionately took sides on the conduct of a distant war and on the demands for power at home of their minorities—the blacks, the women, and the young.

Remembered in this way, it ended in Aristotelian catharsis. Richard Nixon was a doomed anti-hero, whose coerced self-sacrifice, with true irony, realized his campaign slogan in bringing us together. Remembered in this way

Watergate was what we needed.

There was almost exactly one decade between the assassination, in November 1963, and the onset of the resolution in irony, which I take to be President Nixon's declaration, in November 1973: "I am not a crook." Irony is that mode in which the audience understands that truth is the opposite of what is said, although the speaker genuinely believes his words.

I shall not try to itemize everything that happened in those ten American years. As a member of the chorus I was forty-one when they started, fifty-one when they ended, and can recall no other decade like it. The proliferation of dreadful events was so great that each of us will give them different emphases. There was the murder on-camera of Lee Harvey Oswald by Jack Ruby. There were the murders of civil rights workers in the South. There was the killing of Robert Kennedy. There was the killing of Martin Luther King, Jr. Terrorism swept the world, most incredibly in the slaughter of Israeli athletes and Arab commandos at the Munich Olympics.

There was the shooting of twenty-nine prisoners and ten hostages at Attica, the death of Mary Jo Kopechne at Chappaquiddick. There was the killing of Sharon Tate and four others in Hollywood, of 109 Vietnamese civilians at My Lai, of young revolutionaries in a Greenwich Village townhouse by their own bombs, of white students at Kent State by the National Guard, of black students at Jackson State College by state highway police, and the crippling by gunfire of George Wallace.

The natural deaths of the former mighty went relatively unremarked: Winston Churchill, Dwight Eisenhower, Charles de Gaulle, Harry Truman, Lyndon Johnson—and J. Edgar Hoover. The first man chosen to replace Hoover flunked his Senate confirmation hearing, and the man rumored to be next in line was Judge William Matthew Byrne, Jr., just then presiding over a hearing of the Ellsberg case, which was going wrong for the administration.

An institution we thought as untouchable by scandal as the Supreme Court was tarnished by the resignation, under pressure, of Abe Fortas, and by Congress finding first Judge Haynsworth, then Judge Carswell, unfit to replace him. The Vice-President of the country Spiro Agnew, was indicted on criminal charges and then plea-bargained with his colleagues at the Justice Department, resigned, and was fined and disbarred.

There were riots, disruptions of church and campus, the growth of the drug culture, and a great swelling up of civil disobedience, which involved, by the time of the move into Cambodia, uncountable numbers of us, chorus and anti-chorus. There was an actual, unarmed invasion of Washington by 250,000 people. It was, I believe, as I have written before, the time of America's cold civil war.

It would be inaccurate to let that evocation of the decade stand without recalling some of the brighter things. The Woodstock Music Festival was one, perhaps, in August 1969. President Nixon's visit to China in February 1972 was more certainly another. But the finest was the great five-day period, back in 1969 again, that started July 16 with the lift-off of Apollo 11 for the moon. At the climax, on July 20, we watched Neil Armstrong swing down the ladder to the moon's surface. It was thrilling, like V-E Day, like the news of Lindbergh's flight across the Atlantic, which I think I remember, though I was only five years old then.

There was some awe in the moon-landing, too, like the awe we felt when we heard of, but did not comprehend, Hiroshima. And there was a rueful counterpoint, as television brought us, interspersed, the haunting news from Chappaquiddick.

Now let me report a passage of domestic conversation. It took place between my son and me in Barcelona, during Watergate days. It is a measure of how long the affair went on that my family and I could have left for Spain fifteen months after the break-in, and after the chief disclosures of the Senate Watergate hearings, stayed abroad for eight months, and returned to find things still erupting—indictments, sentencings, new evidence, tapes, and the opening of the formal House Judiciary hearings on impeachment. The final Watergate summer was about to start. The resignation was still four months away.

I don't recall the actual date of the Barcelona conversation, or what prompted me to make my curious little speech. Philip was fifteen then. I think we were in the kitchen of our middle-class apartment. We may have been making paella.

"When I was a boy," I told him, "I can remember settling down in bed some nights, and drifting comfortably off to sleep with a wonderful feeling of gratitude that I'd been born American, not Chinese or Bulgarian or something. It must have been my equivalent of what religious children get from saying their prayers—to feel blessed, one of the chosen. America had the best government, the finest roads, the soundest money, the mightiest industry, the greatest resources. We were a free, just, and generous people, good people. We did not lose wars, either. An American was just the best and luckiest thing you could be."

I had never thought of myself as indoctrinated in the way that, say, Catholic children are, but of course I had been, by the daily Pledge of Allegiance at school, by the way our history was taught, by the "Star-Spangled Banner" as it opened games and ceremonies, by a Midwestern girl for a mother and an immigrant father who knew he'd landed in the right place.

Philip heard me out carefully, and his reply was meant to comfort: "Gee, Dad. It must have been nice to feel that way."

And at first I was surprised to think that he never had, and then, knowing that he'd been five and aware when JFK was killed, and growing up since, I wasn't surprised any more.

We were in Iowa—living on our farm outside Iowa City, where I had been teaching at the university for some years and was active in protest and politics— when the Watergate break-in occurred. That was June 17, 1972. Three months later I celebrated my fiftieth birthday, having put an ad in the local paper that began, "It's been a long, hot half-century . . ." and ended by inviting anyone who liked, friend or stranger, to drop by the farm that day to help us cool out. Several hundred people came, some of them bringing (as the ad suggested they might, but only if they felt like it) contributions to George McGovern's presidential campaign.

We gathered on the bank of the lower farm pond, in the bright fall sun, drank some beer and even champagne—if it sounds like an occasion that would have included political banter, it was. But even though my birthday is on September 17, and Liddy, Hunt, and the five burglars had just been indicted on the fifteenth, I don't believe Watergate came up. It still seemed such a minor thing, clumsy, scummy, small-time crud-as-usual. We were too inured to the big shocks to pay much attention to a small one. McGovern had tried using Watergate to attack the opposition, comparing the break-in to Nazi tactics. The Republicans sneered at him for intemperate reference, and I was a little embarrassed for him, agreeing that it was overreaction.

We might have nominated George McGovern, but we never really made him our leader, any more than we believed he could be elected. He was something like Cassandra, whom the populace ignores, and we, his supporters, were a lost- cause bunch: I'd been a Shirley Chisholm delegate to the Johnson County Democratic Convention during that election season.

As to the scandal, there was no feel yet of historic weight, since nothing could touch Nixon. The Bernstein and Woodward stories broke in October, and whatever their effect in Washington, they did nothing to stop the countrywide landslide in November. In January, after the Inauguration, Nixon's Gallup-poll popularity was at an all-time high of 68 percent. In terms of classic tragedy it was the kind of pinnacle from which the mighty fall, but I had no sense of that at all yet. Senator Ervin might be getting ready to investigate, Judge Sirica might declare himself dissatisfied, but my faith in the legislative and judicial check and balance was not stirred from lethargy.

In May, when Haldeman and Ehrlichman and Kleindienst had to resign, when John Dean was fired and a special prosecutor appointed, the Ervin hearings began to play on television. They were fascinating, titillating, a jolly time—still nothing majestic. We went off to Spain that August feeling that some bad guys had been caught for something pretty silly. We read about it through the fall and winter in the *International Herald Tribune*.

When I got home in April 1974, the final Watergate summer was about to begin—things were tenser and more serious. Even so, perhaps because I had seen so many resurrections of Richard Nixon, I could not hope that, with the power of the Presidency supporting him, he would find himself unable to survive in office. It is another irony that inevitability is not apparent while it is operating.

The last thing that I imagined then was that, with retrospect enough, the fallen President would have something more than my sympathy. But let me make the retrospect complete.

I was not aware of Richard Nixon when be first became prominent. In the late forties, when, as a congressman on the House Un-American Activities Committee, he led the charge against Alger Hiss, I did not notice any of the personalities involved other than those of Hiss and Whittaker Chambers. I blocked it out, I guess, as being too damn sad. I was twenty-six, just out of the Army, just married, just published, just graduated from college. There were a lot of identities to be lined up and dressed right, and my political identity—was I a radical or a liberal?—was not in the front rank. (Radical or liberal, in 1948, meant Wallace or Truman; I voted for Truman and have been voting for him ever since.)

But by 1950 Tina and I were established on the West Coast. I was working for the *San Francisco Chronicle*, Tina as a volunteer in Helen Gahagan Douglas's campaign for the Senate. It was then that we became aware that there was some nasty little party out of Southern California named Nixon, selling what we were learning to call "guilt by association," in a successful attempt to misrepresent Mrs. Douglas as pro-Communist. I mention this to support my claim of long standing as a Nixon-hater, though it also shows that there are those who have more seniority. Still, it was a smallish club until the Checkers speech, when Nixon was running for Vice-President. There are two points I want to make in connection with this:

First, the speech and the situation leading to it—Nixon's secret support fund—gave Eisenhower a clear chance to revise the ticket if he had wanted to. He did not want to. That Ike expressed genial satisfaction with his man means one of two things: either he was himself a sucker for the Checkers speech or he saw political value for himself in the mind and character of the man who made it. At this time of reassessment of Dwight Eisenhower's Presidency, much of which seems to be favorable, I want strenuously to object: the anointment of Nixon was a very significant part of Eisenhower's legacy to us—just as, in what deserves heavy emphasis on the final word, part of Nixon's legacy was to have been the placement of Spiro Agnew in the line of descent. Each President, after all, chose the same Vice-President twice.

The second point about my twenty-five years as a Nixon-hater is dubious, obscure, as difficult to express as it is to acknowledge. When I call him the agent of our national catharsis, do I not call myself a Nixon-lover too? We cannot expel, in catharsis, that which is not in us. I am not speaking of something remote and merely symbolic, but of real personal qualities, dark qualities, which he and I always shared. I will choose just one of these:

"I feel ill at ease with the prominent," Nixon said, as quoted by Lou Cannon of the *Washington Post* in an illuminating piece in *The Fall of a President*, a book by the *Post*'s staff. Cannon goes on to quote "a Republican," who said: "Nixon doesn't really have the traits he admires in other men, which is to say he's not strong physically, graceful, coordinated, handsome. He is impressed by people who appear to be tough or know the answers. . . ." Cannon cites a former White House staff member who recalls that Nixon always watched John Connally in Cabinet meetings: "Connally always seemed so sure of himself. The old man liked that. He wanted to be like Connally."

Yes, damn it. I used to watch Connally with exactly the same feeling, though more in fear than admiration. Thinking of him calls up that whole feeling of inadequacy, of being an outsider, of not belonging. A circle is closing: once I felt that way about John Kennedy, with the balance between fear and admiration reversed.

I am speaking, then, of the great American inferiority complex, one of the few items of psychiatric jargon to become a phrase in popular culture. For it, we overcompensate quite splendidly at our best, and maybe cheat and lie a little at our worst.

So I come, at long last, to a sense of brotherhood with Richard Nixon. Marx-brotherhood? No. The comic view of it all is more deeply buried than I realized, and what I took then for the gibbering of partisan clowns I hear now as the cries of the stricken, the weeping of the well-intentioned, and the mourning of the just.

When the chorus, in a Greek choral ode, moved from right to left, the words it spoke were called the strophe. When it moved from left to right, they were called the antistrophe, and my memoir seems to be moving now in that direction. I am moved to many recantations. Let this one stand for all: Martha Mitchell. Was she really the straight woman in a slapstick hour? No, she was actually, long before Bernstein and Woodward's sources, the first person to try to speak out on Watergate, and without prompting, just four days after the break-in. Whatever we understand about what moved her to it, Martha Mitchell called the press to try to tell of "all the dirty things that are going on"—and her telephone was ripped off the wall by one of Pat Gray's FBI men. She was held prisoner, she said during a second call, thrown down and forcibly sedated by a hypodermic to keep her quiet.

No one paid much attention back then, certainly not I. I was too used to taking her for a kind of female Agnew to feel like anything but chuckling.

We watched the final summer, my wife and I, Philip sometimes, through the eyes of Dan Rather at five-thirty every evening. The watching was compulsive and mostly silent. If we talked about it some among ourselves, it was muted. It never did become a lively topic of Iowa conversation, but not because anyone dismissed it any longer. We just didn't expose our feelings, or chance offending those of others. At university parties, after tennis, at the Windham Garage where the farmers met, we spoke of other things and hurried home at network news time. We watched our district representative in Congress, Ed Mezvinsky, who was on the Judiciary Committee, vote for impeachment one day. Though we were friends, I had no will to phone or write to him about it.

It was, I think, because we felt, unconsciously, the time of our division coming to an end. We must not risk, by chattering, hubris, which is the arrogance of setting oneself among the gods. Nixon had risked it for us, and the gods of democracy, known to us through their sacred writings—the Declaration of Independence, the Constitution, and the Bill of Rights—were as inexorable as any. We saw our scapegoat struggle. We watched him go down. And through him came, I now believe, a restoration of faith, a cleansing, and the lifting of an enormous burden.

January 1984

QUESTIONS

1. Was it appropriate for President Ford to pardon Richard Nixon? Was the nation better served by putting Watergate behind us?

2. Are there ever occasions when a President is above the law? Often the President invokes concern for national security as the rationale behind non compliance, does this seem reasonable?

3. Was Richard Nixon an aberration or a creation of American politics? Does the American political system attract individuals with certain personality characteristics?

CHAPTER 12

THE PRESIDENT, THE PEOPLE, AND THE POWER TO MAKE WAR

Eric F. Goldman

As Eric Goldman writes in the following piece, "The wise and hardheaded men who assembled in 1787 to write a constitution for the United States were members of a generation that had just fought a bitter war against the British executive, King George III." Not surprisingly they wanted to avoid future war, and to assure that no one man could take people into war again. Goldman offers this as the reason why the Founding Fathers gave Congress, not the President, the power to make war and peace. He points out though the tension inherent in a system where the Chief Executive takes the lead in foreign policy, yet is beholden to the Congress. Goldman considers the original intention regarding war powers, of our Founding Fathers, and questions if these intentions are still appropriate. He leaves us with the troubling concern expressed by Benjamin Franklin, that is " . . . what sort of human being will end up in the White House?" What if he or she was " . . . overly ambitious or 'fond of war?' "

The Constitution of the United States declares in the plainest possible English: "The Congress shall have Power . . . To declare War." Yet in the last twenty years Americans have fought two major wars—in Korea and in Vietnam—without a congressional declaration of war. Apart from the question of who has the right to send the armed forces into serious combat action, Vietnam has been a glaring instance of momentous foreign policy carried out with only the most cursory control by Congress.

Naturally, many Americans opposed to the Vietnam war are crying outrage. Many others, for or against the war or somewhere in between, ask a worried question: What has happened to the traditional constitutional procedure whereby the President leads in international affairs but Congress has a potent check on him when the decision involves life and death for the nation's young men and sweeping consequences for the whole country? Is there no way to bring foreign policy back under greater popular control, by restoring the congressional role or through some other technique?

On the surface, the questions have clear-cut answers, most of which revolve around the contention that particular recent Presidents simply have refused to play by the constitutional rules. Yet in actuality the answers are entangled in complex considerations of just what the Founding Fathers did and did not write into the Constitution, had their decisions have been put into practice over two centuries, and whether the circumstances of warmaking have not changed so much that some of the basic old rules simply do not apply.

The wise and hardheaded men who assembled in 1787 to write a constitution for the United States were members of a generation that had just fought a bitter war against the British executive, King George III. They were sick of battles and their devastation and intensely concerned to circumscribe any decision for war. A gangling freshman congressman from Illinois, denouncing the Mexican- American War a half century later, stated the mood of most of the Founding Fathers as accurately as any historian can. Representative Abraham Lincoln wrote in 1848 that the Constitutional Convention gave the warmaking power to Congress because "kings had always been involving and impoverishing their people in wars, pretending generally, if not always, that the good of the people was the object. This, our Convention understood to be the most oppressive of all kingly oppressions; and they resolved to so frame the Constitution that *no one man* should hold the power of bringing this oppression upon us." (The italics are Lincoln's.)

So the Congress, not the President, was to decide war or peace. But the Founding Fathers lived in an era filled with violence between countries that was not formal war. The new nation would be at a sharp disadvantage if, in the event of depredations against its commerce or maraudings on its land, its armed forces were immobilized until congressmen could gather from thirteen states in their horse-drawn vehicles. The Founding Fathers made one man who was on the scene, the President, Commander in Chief of the Army and Navy. The wording of the first draft of the Constitution gave Congress the exclusive power to "make" war. On the floor of the convention, "make" was changed to "declare," assigning the President the right to use the Army and Navy in order to meet specific emergencies while retaining for the House and Senate the power to decide full-scale war.

The Constitution has often been called a bundle of compromises, and so it was—not least between those who wanted a strong and those who wanted a weak Chief Executive. The Founding Fathers may have made the President the Commander in Chief, but they gave Congress the power of the purse in determining the size and nature of the armed forces. Until late in the convention, the right to make treaties was vested in the Senate alone. But there were obvious advantages in having one man initiate treaties, receive foreign ambassadors, name and instruct American ambassadors. The Chief Executive would do these things, although he was to appoint ambassadors only with the approval of a Senate majority and make treaties with the "Advice and Consent" of two thirds of the Senate.

In foreign affairs, as in all areas, the Founding Fathers were notably spare in laying down specific dictates and in the language that they used to write the provisions. Yet they said enough to make it clear that they envisaged a foreign policy system in which the President would lead, but in collaboration with Congress, especially the Senate, and in which the Chief Executive would be subject to continuing scrutiny and formidable restraints whenever his activities touched that most serious aspect of foreign affairs, general war.

On August 22, 1789, President George Washington, sound Constitutionalist that he was, appeared with his Secretary of War in the Senate chamber to "advise" with the senators on a treaty with the southern Indians and to seek their "consent." The reading of the document began. The wasp-tempered Senator William Maclay, from the back country of Pennsylvania, was annoyed because the passing carriages made it difficult for him to hear the words; he and other senators, in the process of forming an agrarian political opposition to President Washington, were ready to be annoyed at anything that came from this administration with its "monarchical" tendencies. The President wanted an immediate vote, but the Maclay group called for time to study the documents connected with the treaty. George Washington, according to Maclay, "started up in a violent fret." Had he not brought along the Secretary of War precisely to answer any questions that might arise? President Washington calmed down, the delay was granted, the treaty was ratified. But Maclay wrote in his diary, "The President wishes to tread on the necks of the Senate. . . . This will not do with Americans." As for George Washington, he is said to have let it be known that "he would be damned if he ever went there again." He did not go there again for advice on a treaty, and neither did any other President.

The clash over this minor document was a preview of the coming years, when the collaboration between the Chief Executive and the Congress, in the case of treaties or other aspects of international affairs, proved prickly and at times violent. Inevitably, Presidents tended to feel that they had superior information and were acting only after mature consideration of the matter; congressmen were interfering out of impulse, ignorance, politics, or a yen to encroach on White House prerogatives. Inevitably, congressmen, considering themselves sound in judgment and closer to the popular will, tended to believe that Chief Executives were trying, as Senator Maclay had declared, to create situations in which "advices and consents [would be] ravished, in a degree, from us."

Before many decades it also became clear that while Congress might have the war power, a determined Chief Executive could put the House and the Senate in a position where they had little alternative except to vote war. The Democratic President elected in 1844, the unsmiling, tenacious James K. Polk, believed it was manifest destiny for America to expand. Texas had been formally annexed, but Mexico still considered it a rebellious province, and border disputes continued; California lay a luscious plum ready for the plucking from Mexico. President Polk kept trying to maneuver Mexico into acceptance of his ambitions, while he built a fervid public opinion behind expansionism. Finally the President ordered General Zachary Taylor into territory claimed by Mexico, and Mexican troops attacked American cavalry, killing or wounding sixteen.

On Sunday, May 10, 1846, President Polk went to church but, as he put it, "regretted" that he had to spend the rest of the Sabbath on a quite different matter working out a war bill and a strategy for Congress. The measure provided an appropriation of ten million dollars and the calling up of fifty thousand volunteers. The disciplined Democratic majority in the House of Representatives limited debate to two hours, and only in the last minutes did the Polk leaders present a preamble to the bill that was a declaration of war. The House and the Senate included a strong anti-war faction. But now all members were in the position where they either voted for the whole measure or—with a good deal of public opinion near hysteria—voted against money and troops for General Taylor's forces. The House approved, 174–14; the Senate, 40–2.

Those dogged fourteen Noes in the House included ex-President John Quincy Adams; and Representative Abraham Lincoln, just arrived in Washington, would soon begin his sharpshooting against the war. Major intellectuals joined in the assault. Henry Thoreau spent a night in the Concord lockup for refusing to pay his poll tax in protest, and when his aunt paid the money, much to his annoyance, he went back to Walden Pond and wrote his famous essay "Civil Disobedience." The agitation went on, but within five months American troops were swinging along the plaza of Mexico City, gazing in awe and in triumph at the great baroque cathedral and the pink walls of the Halls of Montezuma, asserting by their mud-spattered presence that President Polk was about to achieve in abundance the territorial acquisitions he sought.

Half a century later the obverse of the coin was showing. Of all wars the United States has fought, none has come to be considered more pointless and reprehensible than the Spanish-American War, and that venture was the doing of Congress, driven on by public opinion. During the 1890s a rebellion in the Spanish colony of Cuba, brutally combatted by the Madrid government, caught up a mounting jingo sentiment in the United States. Before long the principal opponents of armed intervention were the American businessmen owning property in Cuba, who wanted things settled without dislocating their economic arrangements, and the two Presidents of the era, Grover Cleveland and William McKinley.

When Congress roared through a resolution recognizing the "belligerency" of the Cuban rebels, President Cleveland denounced the move as an intrusion on the powers of the Chief Executive and privately remarked that if Congress declared war, he as Commander in Chief would refuse to mobilize the Army. President McKinley tried, too; he undertook negotiations with Madrid to bring better treatment of the rebels. But the popular uproar, stoked by tabloid papers, kept increasing. William McKinley's face grew haggard from the pills he was taking trying to get to sleep; once he sat on a big crimson brocade lounge in the White House and burst into tears as he spoke of the way Congress was forcing the country into war. Finally, the President capitulated. He planned to run for re-election; besides, he was scarcely deaf to voices like that of the senator who thundered to Assistant Secretary of State William R. Day, "Day, by——, don't your President know where the war-declaring power is lodged? Tell him by—— ——, that if he doesn't do something, Congress will exercise the power." President McKinley sat working on a war message as the Spanish government conceded major American demands—a concession made before the message actually reached the House and the Senate—and he added poignantly that he hoped Congress would give the Spanish terms "just and careful attention."

A war of territorial seizure maneuvered through by a determined President, an ugly war forced by public opinion and Congress, six wars or significant uses of the armed forces in a little more than a hundred years, more and more instances of acrid White House—Congress clashes in foreign affairs—during the late eighteenth and nineteenth centuries the constitutional system was hardly functioning with glowing results in international matters. Yet the wars or quasi-wars did not pile up long casualty lists; they did not slash through everyday living. The most disruptive conflict, the Civil War, was removed by its very nature from the usual questions of constitutional responsibility. Whatever the underlying reality, even the Mexican-American War was fought under an authorization overwhelmingly granted by Congress. If the wars created savage debates, they spread little bitter feeling that questions of life and death were too far removed from grass-roots control.

President Theodore Roosevelt has often been called "the first modern President," and he was that in many ways. In international affairs the world was taking on its twentieth-century form of great powers jockeying for global position, vast economic stakes overseas, and armed forces designed to strike swiftly. These trends inevitably centered more foreign policy power in the hands of the American President, who was far more able than the cumbersome Congress to operate in this kind of arena. The rambunctious Teddy Roosevelt, no man to turn away from power, responded by driving deep into the American system the doctrine that the Chief Executive is—to use his phrase—"the steward" of the nation, endowed under the Constitution with vast "inherent powers" to act in behalf of what he considers the good of the country.

Action accompanied doctrine. Did TR deem it to be in the national interest for the United States to have a canal across Central America so that the Navy could be moved quickly from one ocean to another, and was the Colombian government proving balky? In 1903 TR saw to it that Panamanian rebels set up an independent state covering the desired canal zone, and the new nation, to no one's surprise, gave him what he wanted. ("I took the Canal Zone," said President Theodore Roosevelt, "and let Congress debate.") Did TR arrive at the conclusion during the Russo-Japanese War of 1904–05 that the security of the United States was best served by a Japanese victory? In entire secrecy he informed Tokyo that, if needed, America would act as an ally, which could have proved a commitment for war. Did the triumphant Japanese then seem a bit too cocky? In 1907 TR ordered the entire American fleet on a razzle-dazzle trip around the world, loosing all kinds of diplomatic reverberations. Congressional opponents stirred, particularly those from eastern regions fearing the lack of naval protection, and they talked of denying the appropriation for the fleet movement. Very well, TR replied. He had enough money to send the ships to the Pacific Coast, and they could stay there.

It was all very much Teddy Roosevelt, and more than a little rococo. Yet this first modern President was also anticipating in a serious way the modern presidential trend. Stirred on by changed conditions, he was moving through that broad arch erected by the Founding Fathers—between, on the one side, the clear power of the Chief Executive to lead in foreign affairs and to command the armed forces and, on the other side, the powers of Congress to do certain specific things.

As the twentieth century progressed and the enmeshments of the world grew tighter and more troublesome, Presidents probed still more vigorously the limits of the arch. This development was not only implicit in the circumstances; it was furthered by the difference between the vantage of the Chief Executive and the Congress. The President felt full blast the forces of modernity, which came crashing daily into his office. As the leader of the whole nation, he was heavily influenced by considerations of collective security, the moral position of the United States before international opinion, and the problems that tied in with the stability of the country's economy. Of course members of Congress knew these same concerns, but they were also subject to local, more inward-looking pressures. The House and the Senate continued to include strong blocs which represented the decades-old view that the business of America is America and which resented the persistent intrusion of the world. The abrasion between the two ends of Pennsylvania Avenue in matters of foreign policy sharpened. More and more, Presidents viewed Congress as the adversary and thought in terms of skirting around it or, if necessary, ignoring it.

This occurred at critical points on the road toward American participation in both World Wars I and II. During the European phase of World War I, Germany climaxed three years of friction with the United States by announcing unrestricted submarine warfare. President Wilson had long been troubled by considerations of the moral position of the United States with respect to the conflict, and the feeling of his responsibility to assert American rights on the high seas; now he could not overlook the fact that hundreds of ships, fearful of submarines, were clinging to port and great supplies of wheat and cotton were piling up, threatening to dislocate the nation's economic life. In February,

1917, President Wilson asked Congress for authority to arm merchantmen, an act that could scarcely fail to lead to war. The debate was stormy, and in the upper house eleven senators filibustered the measure to death. Thereupon the President announced that "a little group of willful men had rendered the great government of the United States helpless and contemptible" and ordered the merchantmen armed anyhow. War was declared in April.

After the eruption of the second European war in 1939 President Franklin Roosevelt was convinced that for the good of the United States it belonged at the side of the antifascist powers. Yet he faced tremendous anti-intervention sentiment, so amply reflected in Congress that as late as the summer of 1941, a year after the fall of France, the House extended the draft law by exactly one vote. Under the circumstances, FDR undertook an extraordinary series of executive actions, which sought to hem in Japan economically and to help the nations fighting Nazi Germany. Weeks before Pearl Harbor these moves included an order that in effect meant convoying—despite a congressional ban on convoying—and an order to the Army Air Forces and the Navy to shoot first at German and Italian vessels found in the western Atlantic, which amounted to *de facto* warfare.

By the time America was fighting in World War II, it was manifest that President Roosevelt had made war and was continuing to conduct foreign policy with only a defensive concern for congressional opinion. Plenty of angry comment was made about this, yet still the warmaking power did not become a major national issue. In the case of both World Wars I and II, a semblance of congressional authority was preserved by the ultimate declarations of war voted by the House and Senate. Of more significance, the two wars were generally accepted by the public; they were led by widely popular Chief Executives; and if they brought serious problems to the society, they did not seem to tear it apart.

In June, 1950, President Harry Truman was visiting his Missouri home when he learned of the invasion of South Korea by North Korea. Flying back to Washington, he mulled over the news. This was plain aggression, the President told himself; aggression unchecked during the 1930s had led to World War II; he was not going to be party to another such tragedy. The next morning the reports were grim: South Korea appeared about to collapse. That night Harry Truman ordered American armed forces into the Korean fighting. Then the United Nations Security Council, on motion of the United States representative, "recommended" assistance to South Korea, and the President summoned congressional leaders, as he put it, "so that I might inform them on the events and decisions of the past few days." The Korean War was under way, grinding on for more than three years, costing the nation 33,629 battle deaths and 103,284 wounded. At no time did President Truman ask congressional authority for the war.

Behind this White House attitude were all the reasons that had been accumulating for decades. But other and profoundly important elements had also entered into the relationship between the Chief Executive and Congress in the conduct of foreign affairs. The simple fact was that the traditional concept of a President leading in foreign policy and then, if necessary, going to Congress for a declaration of war had become obsolete. Historically, war meant that a nation, using whatever weapons seemed feasible, attempted to conquer another country or to beat it into submission. In an era of Cold War, and after the development of nuclear weapons, armed conflicts were taking a different form. Small Communist nations, unofficially backed by large ones, were probing remote areas. The United States was replying not by war in the conventional sense but by what was being called "limited war"—limited in the use of weapons because nuclear power was ruled out and limited in objective, which was not to crush the enemy but to stop him from spreading Communism and to discourage similar efforts in the future.

All the while, the relationship of war to the home front was altering. By the 1950s the United States was so complex a society and Washington so overwhelming a force that a declaration of war had immense impact. This was partly psychological, but it also involved fundamental workaday facts. Over the decades, by laws and even more by precedents, a declaration of war had come to confer on the President sweeping powers over the entire national life, particularly in the sensitive area of economic affairs. Fighting a limited war, President Truman wanted to limit its home effects, and the opposition to them which could be so easily aroused.

So President Harry Truman went on fighting the Korean War on the authority of President Harry Truman. At times he spoke of the "authorization" or "summons" resulting from the action of the U.N. Security Council; the references were not taken too seriously. The war took calamitous turns. It exacerbated American social problems that were already serious. The very idea of "limited war"—"fighting a war with one hand tied behind you," as people said—ground on the nerves of a nation accustomed to striding in for the knockout. Public opinion, which at first strongly favored the Korean intervention, swung against it and to an extent that had not occurred during any previous conflict; by 1951 the Gallup poll reported a majority believing that the whole intervention was a mistake and favoring prompt withdrawal. Opposition leaders in Congress now were storming against "Truman's War," that "unconstitutional" war; and this time the attacks were building a feeling that something was definitely wrong with the warmaking procedures of the United States.

After the Korean War, and as part of the mounting American concern over Communist expansionism, the United States stepped up negotiations with other nations for regional defense pacts. These agreements were impeccably constitutional; they were treaties, negotiated by the executive branch, then debated in the Senate and approved by a two-thirds vote. Yet they contained clauses that could be construed to give Presidents further leverage in foreign affairs. A typical pact was SEATO, negotiated in 1954 by the Eisenhower Secretary of State, John Foster Dulles. It bound the United States, in the event of "armed aggression" by a Communist nation in Southeast Asia, to "act to meet the common danger in accordance with its constitutional processes" and, in the case of other types of threats in the area, to "consult" on the measures to be adopted—whatever a President might take all that to mean, in whatever specific circumstances he found himself.

Simultaneously, an old procedure—a joint House-Senate congressional resolution concerning international affairs—was gathering fresh meaning. After the lambasting President Truman took during the Korean War, Presidents who contemplated moves that might result in war or quasi-war sought some form of mandate from the House and the Senate. They also wanted to gather bipartisan support behind their action or projected action and behind their general policy, and—of great importance in their minds—they sought to present a united front to warn off Communist or Communist-allied nations from adventurous plans.

The joint resolutions came in rapid succession: in 1955, when President Eisenhower thought he might use armed forces to protect Formosa from Red China; in 1957, when he was considering intervening in the Middle East to prevent strategic areas from falling under Soviet control; and in 1962, when President Kennedy was maneuvering to isolate Castro's Cuba. The joint resolutions varied in a number of ways. But they were alike in their general pattern of giving congressional approval to a specific action or contemplated action of the Chief Executive and to his broadly stated policy for a particular troubled area of the world.

During the presidential campaign of 1964, the celebrated shots were fired in the Gulf of Tonkin by North Vietnamese gunboats against an American destroyer. A heated debate has broken out concerning just how honest President Lyndon Johnson was in reporting the total episode to the public and concerning the larger circumstances surrounding it. The relevant facts here are that the President believed that he should, by retaliating, discourage the North Vietnamese from any such further attacks; that as a politician running for office, he wanted to underline that he was as anti-Communist as his opponent, Barry Goldwater; that the South Vietnamese situation was disintegrating and he did not know what he might want to do about it in the coming months; that he was acutely aware of what had happened to his friend Harry Truman; and that he did not overlook the potentialities of the new type of regional pacts and joint resolutions.

President Johnson ordered a harsh retaliatory bombing of North Vietnamese patrol-boat bases. Then he summoned congressional leaders and told them he thought a joint resolution, like the Formosa and Middle East and Cuban resolutions, should be put through Congress swiftly. The document reached the House and Senate the next morning. It approved the bombing; spoke of America's "obligations" under SEATO to defend South Vietnam; declared that the United States was "prepared, as the President determines, to take all necessary steps, including the use of armed force," to assist any SEATO nation "in defense of its freedom"; and provided that the resolution remain in force until the Chief Executive declared it no longer necessary or the Congress repealed it by majority votes.

The House devoted most of its time to speeches approving the retaliatory bombing of the previous evening, and Representative Henry S. Reuss, from Milwaukee, said all that could be said on that subject. He was reminded, Reuss observed, of the story about the bartender who called the saloon owner on the intercom and asked, "Is Casey good for a drink?"

"Has he had it?"

"He has."

"He is."

The Senate spent more time on the general authorization granted by the resolution. Members rose to ask, Didn't the language mean that the Congress was empowering the President to take any steps he deemed wise, including waging war, in Southeast Asia? Senator J. William Fulbright, the floor leader for the resolution, and a number of other senators replied that President Johnson had stated that it was his policy not to use combat forces in Southeast Asia; the resolution simply backed this policy; it had to be broad and to be approved quickly to show the North Vietnamese how much the American people, without regard to party, were against armed Communist expansion in Southeast Asia. How many congressmen wanted to vote No on such a proposition, especially three months before an election? The debate on the Tonkin Resolution in the House took just forty minutes, and the tally was 416–0. The Senate, after only eight hours of discussion, approved 88–2.

As President Johnson went on escalating the Vietnam war, he brandished freely the foreign policy powers of the White House, including making executive agreements—some secret—that went well beyond the Truman moves and entangled the United States and Asian countries in ways the full purport of which is still not known. More than the Korean War, Vietnam distorted American society at a time when it was still less able to stand further dislocation. And as a large part of public opinion and of Congress turned against the involvement, the cries once again went up, against "Johnson's war," that "unconstitutional horror." But this time there was a difference.

Lyndon Johnson used to carry the difference around with him on a piece of paper crumpled in his pocket. When the subject of his authority for the war came up, he would pull out the slip containing the Tonkin Resolution and read from it. The two Eisenhower joint resolutions and the Kennedy one had concerned crises that went away, or at least seemed to; the problem treated in the Tonkin Resolution turned into a major war, and LBJ exploited the document fully, privately and publicly. On one private occasion, he took it out and read emphatically the resolution's reference to American "obligations" under SEATO. With still more stress, hand clapping on knee, he repeated the phrases that the United States was "prepared, *as the President determines,* to take all necessary steps." Lyndon Johnson demanded to know, Did Congress limit its authorization in *any* way? Embittered by the opposition to the war and the personal attacks on him, he continued in a deliberately provocative allusion to nuclear bombs, which he had no intention of using: Did Congress limit at all even *what kind* of weapons he could use? The President put the paper away. Besides, he added, if they have changed their minds, why don't they just vote, as the resolution says, to repeal it?

Lyndon Johnson knew perfectly well that few congressmen would dare face their constituents if, by such a vote for repeal, they undercut a President and a Commander in Chief in the middle of a grave war which he had entered with the insistence that it was vital to American security and world peace. The new regional pacts and even more the joint resolutions—inaugurated with the best of intentions to meet contemporary circumstances—had given the Chief Executive still more war power, and done it in a manner that came close to caricaturing the intent of the Founding Fathers. For they were nothing less than a means by which Congress, with all the whereases of constitutional procedure, duly voted itself into impotence.

In 1967 President Johnson's Under Secretary of State, Nicholas deB. Katzenbach, appeared before the Senate Foreign Relations Committee. His remarks, reflecting the LBJ mood, came close to saying that the Chief Executive has the right to do anything he considers best in international matters without regard to Congress. Midway in the testimony a committee member, Senator Eugene J. McCarthy, got up and walked out muttering, "There is only one thing to do—take it to the country. This reaction was a factor in projecting McCarthy into his anti-war presidential candidacy. It was a reaction that was being felt throughout the country—combining discontent with the war and what it was doing to the nation with the charge that President Johnson was manipulating and bulldozing the American people through a war they did not want to fight.

Inevitably, a flood of proposals have come, some for amendments to the Constitution, others for congressional action. Almost all seek to return to Congress—and thus, presumably, closer to "the people"—greater participation in foreign affairs, with the usual assumption that the Congress would be less likely to venture into unwise wars than the President. The most serious of these moves has been a resolution proposed by Senator Fulbright and adopted by the Senate in 1969 which went at one major aspect of the problem through the concept of a "national commitment." It was "the sense of the Senate," the resolution declared, that the United States can make a commitment to a foreign nation only through a specific document agreed upon by both the legislative and executive branches.

But serious doubts are provoked by any of these proposals. The nub of the situation is the power of the Chief Executive as Commander in Chief and those general or "inherent powers" that have come to cluster about the office of the Presidency. Is there really a way to restrict the powers of the Commander in Chief without possibly doing more harm than good in an era when one man's swiftly pressing the button may be necessary for some degree of national survival, or his prompt decision to use non-nuclear armed forces could be essential to achieving a purpose generally agreed upon by the country? Do the words exist that could inhibit "inherent powers" without simultaneously harassing the President, or blocking him, in taking actions that are widely considered necessary? Is this not particularly true in a period when his office is the one instrumentality that can make decisive moves in behalf of the national interest, whether that interest be expressed in domestic or foreign affairs—in orders to armed forces to strike abroad or to enforce federal laws at home, to affect importantly the deployment of economic and social resources inside the country or eight thousand miles away, or to assert at home or abroad the nation's bedrock values? Yet if the proposals do not cut back on any of these essentials, how effectively do they close off the routes by which Presidents have moved independently to war?

The Fulbright resolution concerning "national commitments," for example, might discourage certain kinds of the global wheeler-dealing of a Theodore Roosevelt or a Lyndon Johnson. But the resolution is merely an expression of senatorial opinion; it puts no effective check on a Chief Executive acting as Commander in Chief or wielding "inherent powers." Neither TR nor LBJ would have considered the basic moves of their foreign policies subject to the resolution, and almost certainly it would not have prevented American entrance into, say, the Vietnam war.

Apart from the difficulty of controlling the President by new language, there is a still more troublesome question—whether, in fact, the Congress and "the people" are less likely than a Chief Executive to get the country into an unwise war. There is not only the glaring instance of the Spanish-American war; other examples, most notably the War of 1812, give pause. Then a rampant faction in Congress—a group with dreams of conquering Canada, who brought the phrase "war hawks" into the American language—helped mightily in pushing the United States into a conflict that was a credit neither to the good sense nor the conscience of the nation. Similarly, in the early, frightened Cold War days, President Truman was worried, and justly so, about a considerable congressional bloc that was restless to take on Russia.

Yet whatever must be said about the dangers or difficulties of restricting the presidential power to make war, the fact remains that something is decidedly wrong with the process as it has emerged full-blown in the 1960s. It *is* a travesty of democracy to have so vital a decision so completely in the hands of one man. As Benjamin Franklin observed during the Constitutional Convention, the nation can never be sure "what sort" of human being will end up in the White House; some might be overly ambitious or "fond of war." The country can also never be certain—no matter how able and peace-minded the Chief Executive— that he will not be led into an unfortunate decision by his dogmas or his limitations. Lyndon Johnson, to use a striking instance, was a Chief Executive of high abilities in a number of respects; he had a strong personal urge to be a peace President and well-seasoned political reasons for avoiding the travail of war. Yet he escalated the Vietnam intervention relentlessly, lashed ahead by old-style certitudes and an inadequate understanding of the forces at work in Asia.

Ideally, what is needed is the creation in modern terms of a system something like the one envisaged by the Founding Fathers, in which the President would have his powers as Commander in Chief and would lead in foreign policy while being guided and checked to some degree by Congress. Toward that end, no good purpose is served by continuing the practice of congressional joint resolutions in international affairs. Either the resolution must say so little that it does not significantly present a bipartisan front to the enemy, or it must be so sweeping that it hands the Chief Executive a blank check.

Beyond this negative suggestion there are all those difficulties in conceiving of a single congressional move that would better the situation. Probably improvement will have to come not by the beguiling expedient of one action but by slower and more complex changes within the existing relationship. For this purpose it is essential to note that in every instance when the United States has gone through all the prescribed constitutional forms, with the President recommending war and the Congress "declaring" it, the House and the Senate have never really "declared war." Five consecutive times, from the War of 1812 through World War II, what Congress actually did was to recognize an existing state of war, allegedly caused by other nations. This was not simply the result of the natural desire to make the enemy appear the cause of the fighting. More importantly, it reflected the facts that by the time Congress considered a declaration of war, a long train of actions had made combat involvement inevitable or next to inevitable and that, in most instances, the actions had been taken by the White House.

The problem of increasing the participation of Congress in foreign policy therefore involves less the matter of a declaration of war than a continuing role for the legislative branch in the decisions that lead to large-scale military intervention. Thinking along these lines, it is useless to assume that the built-in tension between the White House and the Hill can be removed. Yet changes could be made that would increase the degree of genuine collaboration.

All modern Presidents have called in congressmen to "consult" concerning major foreign policy moves. The vital point is the nature of the "consulting." Is it a session in which the Chief Executive really listens to his guests, or is it one

CHAPTER 13

"WHAT HAPPENED TO AMERICA'S PUBLIC SCHOOLS? NOT WHAT YOU MAY THINK"

Gerald W Bracey

Throughout the second half of the twentieth century, America's public school system has been the object of harsh criticism from many quarters. Educators, academics, and politicians alike have claimed consistently that the public schools are in a state of decline and actually may cause some of the nation's ills. Gerald W. Bracey looks at the state of public education in the United States over the past century and concludes that the real story is not the decline of the public schools but the inability of Americans to agree on the purpose of public education. Bracey points out that, in many ways, the public school system, even with its manifest shortcomings, has been a remarkable success story and is doing a better job today than ever. Before the nation can forge something like a consensus about what the public school system should do, however, Americans first must be able to acknowledge that the system has not been a failure.

At one point in his 1988 book *The Thirteenth Man*, the former Secretary of Education Terrel Bell speaks of the decline of secondary education in America. "If we are frank with ourselves," he writes, "we must acknowledge that for most Americans. . . neither diligence in learning nor rigorous standards of performance prevail. . . . How do we once again become a nation of learners, in which attitudes towards intellectual pursuit and quality of work have excellence as their core?"

With these words Bell echoes two qualities common to educational reformers since World War II: nostalgia and amnesia. They look back through a haze to some imagined golden era of American education when we were "a nation of learners," forgetting that a century ago the high school graduation rate was about 3 percent, and it didn't exceed 50 percent until mid-century, whereas today it is 83 percent (if you include those who receive equivalency diplomas or who drop out but then return for diplomas). They forget, too, that until after World War II it was assumed that no more than 20 percent of American youth could handle a college curriculum at all; now 62 percent of all high school graduates enroll in college the following fall.

Yet our schools have been assailed decade after decade -- in the 1950s for letting America fall behind in the space and weapons races; in the 1960s for not bringing about integration fast enough; and in the 1980s for letting the country down in the global marketplace -- as well as coming under fire from national leaders who have had a strong ideological interest in changing the system.

Not that politicians have been the only tough critics of the schools. Many educators have also attacked their performance with an intensity not directed at any other institution in public affairs. Consider these three comments: "The achievement of U.S. students in grades K-12 is very poor"; "American students are performing at much lower levels than students in other industrialized nations"; and "International examinations designed to compare students from all over the world usually show American students at or near the bottom." These are powerful indictments. As it happens, none of them are true. Yet they are the opening sentences from three consecutive 1993 weekly columns in *The New York Times* by the late Albert Shanker, president of the nine-hundred-thousand-member American Federation of Teachers.

While Shanker might have been more abrasive than most, many within the field of education have shown minimal support for public schools. It is impossible to imagine a Secretary of Defense lambasting the Navy or a Secretary of Commerce chastising American industry for its shortcomings the way Secretaries of Education have demeaned the performance of American public schools. How and why did people in the field arrive at such a view?

The story begins in 1893 with the Committee of Ten on Secondary School Studies, better known simply as the Committee of Ten, which comprised five college presidents and other public school officials. The Committee of Ten was the first in a long line of blue-ribbon commissions set up to examine American education. When it began its work, there was little enough to examine, and indeed its main goal was just to bring some coherence to a system that had hardly any organization or clarity of purpose.

In 1890 we were a nation of 63,056,000, but only 203,000 of some 3,000,000 age-eligible children attended secondary school. This was certainly no nation of learners. In fact the committee's report makes it hard to imagine what the few children enrolled in schools did all day. "As things are now," it states, "the high school teacher finds in the pupils fresh from the grammar schools no foundation of elementary mathematical conceptions outside of arithmetic.... When college professors endeavor to teach chemistry, physics, botany, zoology, meteorology, or geology to persons of eighteen or twenty years of age, they discover that in most instances new habits of observing, reflecting, and recording have to be painfully acquired -- habits which they should have acquired in early childhood. The college teacher of history finds in like manner that his subject has never taken any serious hold . . ."

Why were the children's heads so empty? The educator Ralph Tyler, one of the most prolific writers and innovators the field has known -- he directed the

Center for Advanced Studies in the Behavioral Sciences at Stanford University for a number of years -- looked back in 1974, when he was seventy-two, at what schools had been like in his youth: "What I remember . . . are the strictness of discipline, the catechismic type of recitation, the dullness of the textbooks, and the complete absence of any obvious connection between our classwork and the activities we carried on outside of school.... The view held by most teachers and parents was that . . . [the school's] tasks should be sufficiently distasteful to the pupils to require strong discipline to undertake them and carry them through." One might wonder how any scholars at all emerged from such an environment.

After the Committee of Ten's 1893 report, secondary education expanded rapidly, but it remained in disarray as educators debated what the curriculum should look like. *The School Review*, the principal journal of secondary education at the time, was filled with titles cast as questions: "What Should the Modern Secondary School Aim to Accomplish?"; "What Studies Should Predominate in Secondary School?"

As educators attempted to find answers, they didn't even consider an issue that dominates current discussions: the ultimate goal of secondary education and its connection to career. Few students graduated from high school then, and far fewer went on to college, yet the secondary curriculum's main aim was to provide courses acceptable to institutions of higher education. The Committee of Ten backed a high school curriculum aimed solely at preparing students for college....

Furthermore, there was no thought at the time of any vocational role for schools. They had been recognized as ladders up the scale of individual economic well-being, but no one seems to have thought of them as important to the broader well-being of the nation. Too few people attended them for that.

Between 1910 and 1945 secondary schools expanded rapidly, the graduation rate rising from 10 percent to 45 percent. Their growth did not, however, mean any greater coherence. In 1932 the Progressive Education Association noted that secondary education "did not have a clear purpose . . . it did not prepare students adequately for the responsibilities of community life.... The high school seldom challenged the student of firstrate ability, . . ." and "the relation of school and college was unsatisfactory to both institutions."

Criticism of the schools was always abundant during this period, but nobody was yet saying that they had gotten worse; more than anything else, people complained about inefficiency.... The few studies that actually looked at academic results found them wanting, but their authors did not seem inclined to blame the schools. In 1943 *The New York Times*, with the help of the history department of Columbia University, investigated students' knowledge of American history and geography. It found the results appalling: "A large majority of the students showed that they had virtually no knowledge of elementary aspects of American history. They could not identify such names as Abraham Lincoln, Thomas Jefferson, Andrew Jackson or Theodore Roosevelt.... Most of our students do not have the faintest notion of what this country looks like. . . .

Hundreds of students listed Walt Whitman as being an orchestra leader."

The Times didn't see the implication of what surely was the most damning aspect of its findings: The study had been conducted on college freshmen. At the time, about 45 percent of students graduated from high school, and about 15 percent of those graduates went on to college. Thus the survey had uncovered not just ignoramuses but an elite of ignoramuses.

The Times put the story on page one, next to its major headline of the day, PATTON ATTACKS EAST OF EL GUETTAR. It described the study as an effort to learn how much material absorbed in secondary school was retained in college, apparently assuming that the students had once known the material and simply   forgotten   it.

But after World War II the educational failings of students began increasingly to be blamed on the schools, and the first declarations that things had once been better were sounded. The criticism eventually grew so chronic and intense that in 1989 the eminent education historian Lawrence Cremin looked back in perplexity: "The popularization of American schools and colleges since the end of World War II has been nothing short of phenomenal, involving an unprecedented broadening of access, an unprecedented diversification of curricula, and an unprecedented extension of public control. In 1950, 34% of the American population twenty-five years of age or older had completed at least four years of high school, while 6 percent of that population had completed at least four years of college. By 1985, 74% of the American population twenty-five years or older had completed at least four years of high school, while 19% had completed at least four years of college. During the same 35 year period, school and college curricula broadened and diversified tremendously.... Yet this [expansion of schooling] seemed to bring with it a pervasive sense of failure. The question would have to be 'Why?' "

The answer lies in part in the very success schools have had at providing nearly universal secondary education. By the end of the war, secondary school enrollments approached 90 percent. A conference was held in 1945 to discuss how to cope with this expanding clientele. At the time, educators were strongly influenced by the emerging field of psychometrics -- aptitude, achievement, and intelligence testing. Many test makers believed that intellectual ability was inherited and was distributed throughout the population in a normal curve. On the basis of this assumption, the conference decided that no more than 20 percent of high school students would ever go to college. Another 20 percent could be served by the recently developed vocational programs. That left 60 percent of students with no appropriate curriculum.

The conference decided to build a curriculum for this "forgotten 60 percent" around the "needs of students," and this led to the development of what was called Life Adjustment Education.... Liberal arts universities had already looked down on schools of education. When these schools now started promoting Life Adjustment Education, the liberal arts professors exploded in derision. Foremost among these critics was Arthur Bestor, a professor of history at the University of

Illinois, who in 1953 wrote a popular book titled *Educational Wastelands: The Retreat From Learning in Our Public Schools*. Note the word retreat. This appears to be the first time a critique of the schools harked back to a previous time when things were better.

Bestor loaded *Wastelands* with statistics to demonstrate the schools' decline. He observed, for instance, that "fifty years ago, half of all students in public schools were studying Latin; today less than a quarter . . . are enrolled in courses in all foreign languages put together." He failed to add that fifty years before, only 50 percent of students had been enrolled in any school and only 7 percent of all students graduated from high school. A quarter of the current crop of students was actually far more of them.

Thus the sense of failure actually reflected the success of the schools in reaching out to what were called "new learners." But, perhaps more important, it also reflected America's changed role in the world. The Cold War and the space and weapons races were heating up. According to the Committee on the Present Danger, a group of thirty-three powerful leaders from business, industry, the military, and universities, in 1951, "We need both a reservoir of trained men and a continuing advance on every scientific and technical front."

The most vocal advocate of an educated work force as the front line in the Cold War was Adm. Hyman G. Rickover, the father of America's nuclear navy. "Let us never forget," Rickover said, "that there can be no second place in a contest with Russia and that there will be no second chance if we lose." Armed with statistics from the Director of Central Intelligence, Allen Dulles, Rickover stumped the country and harangued members of Congress on the need for more scientists, engineers, and mathematicians. The Russians, Dulles said his statistics showed, were outstripping us in these vital areas.

Where would we get the manpower we needed? Where else but from the schools? For the first time, schools were expected to play a role in national security. And they weren't good enough at it.

When the Russians launched Sputnik, the first man-made satellite to circle the globe, the schools' critics took the event as proof that they had been right. The schools were failing. Sputnik went up in October 1957; by the following spring *Life* magazine had readied a five-part series, Crisis in Education. The cover of the March 24, 1958, edition showed two students: a stern-looking Alexei Kutzkov in Moscow and a relaxed, smiling Stephen Lapekas in Chicago. Inside, photographs showed Kutzkov conducting complex experiments in physics and chemistry and reading Sister Carrie out loud in English class. Lapekas was depicted walking hand in hand with his girlfriend and rehearsing for a musical. In the one American classroom picture, Lapekas retreats from a math problem on the blackboard, laughing along with his classmates. The caption explains that "Stephen amused the class with wisecracks about his ineptitude."

Life engaged Sloan Wilson, author of *The Man in the Gray Flannel Suit*, a successful novel that had become known as something of a social critique, for a two-page essay titled "It's Time to Close Our Carnival." Like Bestor, Wilson saw only decline and failure. "The facts of the school crisis are all out and in plain sight and pretty dreadful to look at," he wrote. "A surprisingly small percentage of high school students is studying what used to be considered basic subjects. ... People are complaining that the diploma has been devaluated to the point of meaninglessness.... It is hard to deny that America's schools, which were supposed to reflect one of history's noblest dreams and to cultivate the nation's youthful minds, have degenerated into a system for coddling and entertaining the mediocre."

In 1983 the government study *A Nation at Risk* would discover a "rising tide of mediocrity." Wilson had found the same swelling current almost precisely twenty-five years earlier. But when Wilson was writing, precious little data existed about school performance, and what there was contradicted the novelist's message. Although the number of people taking the SATs had increased from 10,654 in 1941 to 376,800 in 1957, their scores had remained at the same levels as in 1941, the year SAT standards had been set. And scores on achievement tests had been steadily rising.

American schools have often been faulted for not solving social problems, and in the sixties they were condemned for failing to achieve racial integration soon enough. While they were taking the blame for continued segregation, the verdict arrived on the grand curriculum reforms that had followed Sputnik: They had failed.

Reformers held out great hopes for the new math and its attendant innovations in other fields. That the new curricula were being developed by some of the finest minds at some of our finest universities was initially thought to be their greatest strength. Later it was recognized as their greatest weakness. Although eminent in their fields, the scholars had no sense of how a classroom works....

At about the same time as the new curricula were being pronounced dead, a spate of books was appearing with titles like *Death at an Early Age*, *36 Children*, and *The Way It Spozed to Be*. The antischool feeling was summed up in Charles Silberman's authoritative book *Crisis in the Classroom*.

Crisis in the Classroom appeared in 1970. The red menace still hung over our heads. Domestic events -- assassinations, Vietnam, urban uprisings, Chicago, Kent State -- had created the sense that nothing was secure. In this milieu Silberman observed the malaise that pervaded our schools and wondered why. He pointed out that in a review of 186 then-and-now studies (which compare achievement at two points in time) devoted to education, all but 10 had favored now. He asked, "Why, then, the pervasive sense of crisis? How to explain the fact that an educational system that appears to be superbly successful from one standpoint appears to be in grave trouble from another?" He clearly had the social unrest of both urban blacks and suburban whites in mind when he suggested that "the question cannot be answered with regard to education alone; it is in fact the central paradox of American life. In almost every area, improvements beyond what anyone thought possible fifty or twenty-five or even ten years ago have produced anger and anxiety rather than satisfaction."

But improvements in schools, Silberman concluded, did not mean there was no crisis: "The test of a society, as of an institution, is not whether it is improving, although certainly such a test is relevant, but whether it is adequate to the needs of the present and of the foreseeable future. Our educating institutions fail that test." Thus he rejected nostalgia but saw a crisis nonetheless in the appalling quality of life in schools.

"Because adults take the schools so much for granted," he wrote, "they fail to appreciate what grim, joyless places most American schools are, how oppressive and petty are the rules by which they are governed, how intellectually sterile and aesthetically barren the atmosphere, what an appalling lack of civility obtains on the part of teachers and principals, what contempt they consciously display for children as children."

However accurate Silberman's characterization may have been, it fitted well with the descriptions found in many of the other books of the time. Silberman offered as a cure the same prescription that the journalist Joseph Featherstone had suggested three years earlier in a series of articles that ran in *The New Republic*: open education, a British import that involved making the classroom more informal and that was originally intended only for five-to seven-year-olds.

Whatever currency Silberman's message had was lost seven years later when the College Board called attention to what was then a little-attended fact: SAT scores had been falling for fourteen years. The board formed a panel, headed by former Secretary of Labor Willard Wirtz, to study the decline, and the panel attributed most of it to changes in who was taking the test: more women, more minorities, more students with low high school grades. Noting that the decline stemmed largely from easier access to college, the vice-chair of the panel, former U.S. Commissioner of Education Harold Howe II, wrote an article titled "Let's Have Another SAT Decline." He contended that the civil rights agenda of equal acces to education was unfinished, that the doors needed to be opened wider, and if this caused the scores to drop further, so be it.

The Wirtz panel emphasized the complexity of the decline. One of its background papers simply listed the number of hypotheses brought forward to explain the fall: There were eighty-seven of them, not including one from a physicist blaming the radioactive fallout from nuclear testing programs in the fifties. The media and the public had a simpler interpretation. While the developers of the SAT still called their test a "mere supplement," the public now saw it as the platinum rod for measuring school performance. And that performance was getting worse.

Beginning in 1980 a new diagnosis of what was wrong with American schools appeared, and a new prescription was produced for curing the ailment. Policy papers written for the presidential candidate Ronald Reagan concluded that American schools were declining at the hands of a force heretofore seen as positive in public education: the federal government. Building on arguments made by Milton Friedman in his 1962 book *Capitalism and Freedom*, Reagan's advisers recommended abolishing the U.S. Department of Education, which only recently had been elevated to cabinet status. In addition, tuition tax credits and vouchers should be provided to parents to permit them to choose where to send their children to school. In the free-market environment that would then develop, good schools would flourish and bad schools would go out of business. Previous perceptions of educational decline had led to increased federal involvement. That involvement, the new view contended, had been part of the problem.

In his book about life with a boss who is trying to do away with your job, Reagan's Secretary of Education, Terrel Bell, reports that he heard constant criticisms about the state of American education and began to long for an event that, like Sputnik, would shake the nation out of its complacency. No such event was forthcoming, and Bell fell back on establishing yet another blue-ribbon panel, the National Commission on Excellence in Education.

The commission's report, *A Nation at Risk*, may well rank as one of the most selective uses of data in the history of education. After its opening statement about the "rising tide of mediocrity" and how if an unfriendly foreign power had foisted our schools on us we might have considered it an act of war, the document goes on to list thirteen indicators of dangerous trouble. These indicators seem to have been carefully picked to give as negative a view as possible.

For instance, one of them is: "There was a steady decline in science achievement scores of U.S. 17-year-olds as measured by national assessments of science in 1969, 1973 and 1977." This statement, as far as it goes, is true. But why seventeen-year-olds? Why science? Because only the trend of science scores for seventeen-year-olds supports the crisis rhetoric. The science scores of the other two age groups measured, nine- and thirteen-year-olds, do not. The reading and math scores of nine-, thirteen-, and seventeen-year-olds do not; they were either steady or rising. Of nine trend lines, only one supported the crisis rhetoric. That was the one the commission reported.

The findings should have been challenged by educational organizations, but they had their own reason to accept them: Often their policies are influenced by how an event will affect the availability of funds. Since *A Nation at Risk* depicted grave problems, it seemed likely to generate money to fix those problems. Educational organizations accepted the report enthusiastically.

Risk embraced a new and powerful assumption: that the schools are tightly linked to the performance of the U.S. economy and our ability to compete in the global marketplace. In fact, competition in the global marketplace became the goad for the eighties that the Cold War had been three decades earlier. When a recession arrived late in 1990, this putative link allowed people to blame the schools.

Starting three years ago, however, newspaper headlines began heralding a recovery, and the Geneva-based World Economic Forum pronounced the U.S. economy the most competitive of any among twenty-five developed nations in both 1994 and 1995. In 1996 the forum changed its formula and the United States fell to fourth place; the International Institute for Management and Development retained a formula similar to the forum's old one and found the country still number one. Larry Cuban, a professor at Stanford University, has pointed out that though people blamed schools for the recession of the late eighties, they gave them no credit for the recovery of the nineties, and he dismisses the idea of a strong direct link between educational and economic performance in advanced nations. He points out, for example, that critics of American public education generally argue that Germany and Japan have superior schools. Yet in recent years those two countries have been mired in long-term recessions, their worst since World War II.

Meanwhile the debate over schools and their relationship to the economy has been accompanied by a shift in talk about the purposes of schooling. The goals of building citizens or broadly educated or well-rounded adults have been left behind in favor of the need to prepare students to get jobs and to provide skilled workers for business.

People have never agreed about the purpose of education in this country -- or anywhere else. Aristotle already knew why when he observed that education dealt with "the good life" and people would always differ on what the good life was. To see it principally in terms of getting and keeping a job, though, is rather new to America.

One of our pre-eminent educational influences, Thomas Jefferson, saw education as having two purposes. On one hand, it would act as a great sorting machine with which "the best geniuses will be raked from the rubbish annually" to form an "aristocracy of worth and genius," as opposed to the aristocracies of blood that afflicted Europe. On the other hand, Jefferson thought, all citizens' "minds must be improved to a certain degree" so they could protect the nation from the "germ of corruption."

Even Jefferson's more practical peer Benjamin Franklin did not support vocational training. He realized that people building a new nation would need many skills, but he believed a school's job was to leave them "fitted for learning any business calling or profession." In this he sounds surprisingly like former Secretary of Labor Robert Reich contending that the most valuable skill to learn in school today is "flexibility." In any case, specific vocational goals entered educational discussions early in this century, as secondary schooling began its rapid expansion. When *A Nation at Risk* appeared, it emphasized the preparation of a skilled work force as no one had before.

A Nation at Risk has served the purposes of both those who want to provide more resources for the schools and those who want to overhaul the system and introduce privatization. Both sides have appeared to welcome only bad news about the schools. Thus, when a large, federally funded report concluded that there was no crisis in American education, the Bush administration suppressed it; it was ultimately published by the Clinton administration under the title *Perspectives on Education in America*. And the Bush Department of Education held a press conference to publicize an international study that found American students ranking low in math and science (the distinction between "ranks" and "performance" is critical; the eighth-fastest human being on the planet ranks dead last in the finals of the hundred-meter dash at the Olympics) but made no attempt to tell anyone when another study found American students' reading skills the second best of any of thirty-one countries. That study was eventually discovered by *Education Week*; when *USA Today* subsequently reported it, the paper also quoted a deputy Assistant Secretary of Education dismissing the finding.

In 1993 former Secretary of Education William Bennett released numbers purporting to show that there is no relationship between states' SAT scores and the money those states spend on education. This report was widely disseminated by the Heritage Foundation, and the table summarizing its results was reproduced in *The Wall Street Journal*. Yet people have known for years that the principal source of differences among states lies in the proportion of seniors taking the SAT. In Utah and Mississippi only 4 percent of the seniors take the test, and this tiny elite does well. In Connecticut, which spends far more per pupil on education, 81 percent of the senior class huddles in angst on Saturday mornings to fill in the answer sheets. With the vast majority of its seniors taking the test, Connecticut is digging much deeper into its talent pool, and that excavation shows up in lower scores.

Whether elements of free-market competition would improve schools is not a question for this article, but it seems clear that those who support the notion have sometimes been overzealous in their search for evidence that the current system does not work. The resulting stream of negativity has created a climate in which the media accentuate the negative, sometimes inaccurately.

For instance, in 1993 the usually reliable *Education Week* conducted a ten-year retrospective on what had happened since *A Nation at Risk* appeared. The answer, essentially, was not much: The "proportion of American youngsters performing at high levels remains infinitesimally small. In the past ten years for instance the number and proportion of students scoring at or above 650 on the verbal or math section of the Scholastic Aptitude Test has actually declined." But the numbers that confirmed the fall were for scores between 650 and 800 in 1982 but only for scores between 650 and 690 in 1992. When the higher scores were added in for the later year, they showed clearly that, in fact, more students were doing well than ever.

In the three years since, the proportion of high scorers has continued to rise. Denis Doyle, a Heritage Foundation visiting fellow, voiced a popular belief in *Issues '96: The Candidate's Briefing Book, 1996*, when he ascribed the rise in scores to Asian-American students. It is true that Asian-American students score much higher on the math SAT than do other ethnic groups, but they cannot account for most of the growth. In fact, there has been a 74 percent rise in the proportion of students scoring above 650 since 1981. Omit Asian students, and you still see a 57 percent increase.

Today most statistics continue to show what Silberman found twenty-five years ago: Now is better than then. Achievement-test scores are at record levels, and the number of students taking advanced-placement exams continues to rise even though the number of students has declined since the peak of the baby boom. Seven of the nine trends in reading, mathematics, and science tracked by the National Assessment of Educational Progress are at all-time highs. Factor out demographic changes in who takes the SAT, and there remains a small decline in verbal scores and none at all in math. And as noted earlier, the proportion of students scoring above 650 on the SATs is at an all-time high, and U.S. students are near the top in reading. The Third International Mathematics and Science Study of 1997, the largest and most sophisticated of the international studies in mathematics and science -- our allegedly weakest areas -- has found that among forty-one nations, American students are average to above average. Students in suburban schools measured alone ranked anywhere from first to fifth among nations, depending on age and subject.

The biggest threat to the American educational system may come not from within our schools but from the depth of our divisions over what exactly they should accomplish and how best to get them to accomplish it. And our divisions will not be healed as long as we ignore the history of the accomplishments that have already been made. We should begin improving our schools by appreciating how well they have, in most places and at most times, done so far.

November 1997

Questions:

(1.) The ideal of universal public education is deeply rooted in American history. Why might it be important to have a national public education system, as opposed to a system made up mostly of private schools of many different types? Would the nation be any worse off if it scaled back its commitment to public education?

(2.) What should be the primary purpose of public school education – to prepare graduates for a specific vocation or profession so they are able to play a productive part in the economy, or to produce competent and well-rounded citizens who help nourish democracy?

(3.) Public schools often have been blamed for failing to solve the nation's social problems. Do you see schools as problem-solving institutions, or as indicators of whether the country is
doing certain things well or poorly at a particular time?